Fi

er this date

-2 JU

14 JAI

14 JAN

20 MAR 2003

25 FEB 2000   27 OCT 2003

17 MAR 2000   15 JAN 2004

-7 APR 2000   26 JAN 2004

12 MAY 2000   03 FEB 2004

13 DEC 2000   18 FEB 2004
               30 SEP 2004
19 MAR 2001   15 NOV 2004

28 MAR 2001

-7 MAR 2002

Practical Eventing

Revised Edition

David O'Connor on On A Mission

Practical Eventing

Revised Edition

by Sally O'Connor

With a Foreword by David O'Connor

Half Halt Press, Inc.
Boonsboro, Maryland

Practical Eventing, Revised Edition
©1998 Sally Ann O'Connor

Published 1998 in the United States of America by
Half Halt Press, Inc.
P. O. Box 67
Boonsboro, MD 21713

Illustrations © 1998 Diann Landau

Photo credits as noted

Printed in the United States of America

First edition, 1980
Second edition, 1984
Third printing, 1987
Fourth printing, 1990
Revised edition, 1998

Library of Congress Cataloging-in-Publication Data

O'Connor, Sally.
    Practical eventing / by Sally O'Connor ; with a foreword by David
O'Connor. -- Rev. ed.
        p.   cm.
    ISBN 0-939481-52-9
    1. Eventing (Horsemanship)   I. Title.
SF295.7.O36   1998
798.2'4--dc21
                                                                98-44329
                                                                CIP

TABLE OF CONTENTS

FOREWORD

When first asked by my mother to write a foreword for the revision of her book *Practical Eventing*, I was nervous at the idea of a son writing a foreword for his mother. Then I realized I was the perfect person, not for the success that I have enjoyed, but because I truly was the first person to benefit from my mother's practical ideas for the preparation of horse and rider for the sport of combined training. My mother's sound ideas, based on classical education with every day applications, are laid out so that anybody preparing for their first event or three-day can understand what it will take to have a safe and enjoyable competition.

I am fortunate to travel all over the country and people are always coming up to me and saying **Practical Eventing** was the first equestrian book they owned and that it was their textbook for years. Truly a handbook for the eventing enthusiast, my mother's step by step explanation of the tasks needed to attain a successful competition are a requirement for any "first timer." This book is a must for all equestrian libraries. I hope you will get a tremendous amount of "practical" knowledge out of it.

I know that I did.

David O'Connor

ACKNOWLEDGEMENTS

The original version of this book was written with the support and encouragement of Ivan Bezugloff of *Dressage and CT* magazine, most of the material appeared in a series of articles published in the magazine.

The United States Combined Training Association published subsequent versions of the paperback. I am grateful for their support. With the changes that have taken place in the sport and the modernization of the rules over the past 18 years it was obvious that an updated version of the book was needed. Beth Carnes of Half Halt Press, who has become a dear friend over the years, agreed to publish this revised edition.

David was a young Pony Club rider at the time the original manuscript was written, and he and his brother Brian were the "guinea pigs" for most of the training methods outlined in the book. I am grateful to both of them for listning to their Mother. David has gone on to be an international event rider and Olympic medalist and has written the Foreward for this new edition.

Not only the text but the photos were quite out of date and Julie Jones patiently came out and shot numerous pictures to illustarate some new ideas. My friends and students in Utah participated with good humor in setting good and bad examples and Pam Olsen provided some needed stadium photos.

A vast literature is already in existence on all facets of riding but it is still hard to find books that relate to the backyard horse, or the difficult horse ridden by amateurs who have no readily available instructor. The highly trained horse in competition had to start somewhere and you can be sure that the way to the top was filled with setbacks and frustrations. I hope this book offers some practical advice to those who would like to get involved. I have been gratified by all the people who have come to me over the years to tell me that a copy of **Practical Eventing** guided them successfully through their first three-day event.

I owe a lasting debt of gratitude to my friend and teacher Lockie Richards who taught me to enjoy riding and competing and provided a New Zealand connection that has grown and lasted over the years.

And to all the horses—who are the real stars in this sport—I offer my thanks.

A young 4 year old prospect, with nice overall balance.

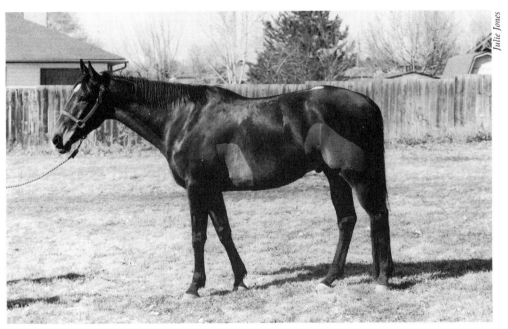

This horse does not appear very strong behind and is too much on the forehand.

PART I:
Preparing for the First Competition

1

THE HORSE

All sports have superstars, those athletes who win consistently through abundant natural ability. But there are also those who succeed because they take the time and effort needed to prepare themselves logically, thoroughly, and systematically. With correct training, anyone can have a shot at the top. This is equally true in combined training or eventing.

The keystone to success is the attention paid to the basic groundwork for all three separate phases. Those who do their homework have the edge when it comes to actual competition. This book plans to take you, step by step, through a basic system of preparing a horse for three-phase competition beginning with the work required before you enter your first Novice competition on up to the more advanced skills needed for your first serious, full three-day event. This won't happen overnight. It takes at least 18 months to progress up to the Preliminary Level and, with your first horse, it is well to plan for two full years.

The first thing to consider is, of course, the horse itself. What kind of horse is best suited to this work? Almost any type of horse can be used for eventing. Many different breeds have been successful, particularly in the lower levels. Event horses come in all different shapes and sizes, and any horse with reasonable conformation can be expected to perform well at the lower levels. Indeed, some of the big names in eventing would never be called back in the show ring.

The ideal horse would be a four- or five-year-old Thoroughbred or three-quarter-bred which has been lightly ridden, perhaps hunted for a season, standing between 16 and 16.3 hands with good bone, a sloping shoulder and, above all, strong hindquarters.

A very rough looking customer. But power in the back end. A bit long in the back, but covers ground effortlessly. You can't always rely on a pretty coat you have to look at the essentials. Eventing is not a conformation competition.

When considering a horse for event work, the hindquarters should be your first concern. The motor is in the back; without this "power plant" you will have nothing. Are the hind legs strong, with good angulation? Are the hocks well-formed? Are the legs straight when viewed from behind? We would all like to own good-looking, "pretty" horses, but don't be beguiled by a pretty head and forget the rest.

Any horse you are considering for eventing should have good, strong, clean legs. They are going to take a good bit of strain and must be up to it. Ideally, the horse should cover a great deal of ground at the canter or gallop. It should float over the ground, eating up the distance effortlessly. Horses that have short, choppy strides, or ones that thud into the ground with each step, take a great deal out of themselves in endurance work and will tire more quickly.

Of vital importance is the cardio-respiratory system. Is the horse built with enough "heart room?" The heart is the pump that keeps everything else working and must be strong enough to provide the energy for the other systems. The lungs must be in good working condition and big enough to provide the vital oxygen. A horse with suspect wind or a heart murmur is not a good prospect. Any horse you intend to event should undergo a thorough veterinary inspection. It must be sound in "eye, wind, limb and heart."

It's a good idea to have your vet do a blood count before you begin working the horse. Sometimes such tests turn up unseen problems that can be more easily corrected at this point than later, when they might become more serious. The teeth should be examined and floated if need be. If your horse's teeth are sharp, they may not be able to grind up feed sufficiently and the horse may not be getting all the goodness out of the food you are stuffing into it.

An event horse must have a temperament that is both generous and somewhat aggressive. A horse that needs to be pushed for each step will never give you that all-important edge needed in competition. Many top event horses are notoriously difficult to ride, but in competition they have that little extra that makes them great instead of merely good. There is a fine line, however, between keenness and hysteria. The easily excitable, highly-strung horse who throws wing-dings at the drop of a hat may never settle down enough to get to work. The two should not be confused. There seems to be a vogue for big horses nowadays. But a horse can be too big for its own good. Many horses who reach 17 hands or more tend to be clumsy and less

Julie Jones

Small quarter horse mare, with rather weak hindquarters. Successful at Training Level.

Julie Jones

This Thoroughbred has competed in hunter/jumper classes and is now succesful at Training level. He is a bold jumper!

able to handle tight distances and tricky places. As one veterinarian puts it, "Horses just aren't meant to be that big. Nature never intended the horse to reach 17 hands. I've seen more problems develop in the bigger horses than in the average 16 hands horse."

There have been several top horses who have been exceedingly small. Grasshopper, who won a Bronze medal for the United States when ridden by Mike Page, was a mere 15 hands. Marcus Aurelius, ridden by Mary Anne Tauskey in the Pan-American Games, the Montreal Olympics, and the 1978 World Championships in Lexington, Kentucky, was affectionately known as "The Bionic Pony." He stood just over 15 hands. Charisma, ridden by Mark Todd of New Zealand, stood just 15.3 hands, but this did not prevent him from winning individual gold medals at *both* the Los Angeles and Seoul Olympic Games. But these are the exceptions, since most smaller horses do not have sufficient ground-covering ability to make it in the big time.

Eventing is really divided into two separate sports: horse trials, which are competitions that take place on one or two days with cross-country courses of up to three miles, and full-scale three-day events, which can have endurance tests of up to 17 miles. As your training and competing progress, you will be able to judge for yourself just where the limits of your particular horse happen to be.

The horse's balance is all important. Does it carry itself evenly on all four legs? Most horses are slightly one-sided, just as people are right- or left-handed, but some are very crooked to start with. This is hard to correct and makes for problems later on.

Having considered the horse and having decided to get started on a training program, you must then consider yourself. How fit are *you?* Eventing is hard work, and there no point in getting your horse well-conditioned and ready to go if you are out of shape. Riding every day helps, but there is no way you can be fit enough without paying some attention to a fitness program. Jogging seems to be the universal exercise, but it has one decided minus: if you jog regularly, you may develop such large calf muscles you won't fit into your boots any longer. Jumping rope can be done at home and improves the wind and limb satisfactorily but, again, those muscles get big quickly. The Royal Canadian Air Force Program is a fine one which can be carried out at home without any special equipment and only takes about 12 minutes a day. There are books available on fitness programs, including ones designed especially for riders, such as **The Total Rider: Health & Fitness for the Equestrian** by Tom Holmes, from this publisher.

Whatever you decide to do, do it faithfully. Competition is grueling and you want to have that extra reserve that can make or break your performance. You will find that as your horse gets fitter, you must keep pace yourself in order to be able to cope.

Eventing is the most demanding of all equestrian sports, requiring an all-around ability. It can also be the most exhilarating and rewarding. The discipline of the dressage ring, the thrill of the cross-country and the challenge of the more formal stadium jumping all require tremendous concentration and sustained effort from you and your partner, the horse. If you have taken the time to prepare, it can be a real thrill. It's a great deal of work, but the result is worth every bit of it.

2

LUNGEING AND FLAT WORK

Lungeing is a vital part of your early training of the horse. It is not, as many people think, just a way of getting the edge off the horse before you ride. Good trainers know that all horses benefit from lunge work, provided it is done correctly.

The equipment required includes a lunge line, a long whip, side reins, a snaffle bridle, a lungeing cavesson, and a saddle. If you feel a proper cavesson is beyond your means, you can lunge off a halter, but keep in mind that this is not as effective as it tends to slip. The cavesson has the advantage of staying still on the horse's head and it also affords you more control. Inexperienced trainers should not attempt to lunge directly from the bridle as it can lead to serious abuse of the horse's mouth.

The side reins should be attached to the girth on each side. They should never be used to force the horse's head into position. Ideally, when the horse carries its head correctly, they will have only a minimum contact. Forcing the head down with tight side reins gives an artificial head carriage and constricts the horse, pulling it behind the bit.

Your horse has to learn to walk, trot and canter on command. Start your work in an enclosed space; if nothing else is available, create a lungeing "ring" by using jumps or cavaletti and two corners of a field or fenced-in paddock. Not everyone has a convenient indoor school, but with a little ingenuity you can come up with some kind of temporary barrier. Why? Because if you don't and your horse decides to take off, you will find yourself either being pulled along the ground at the end of the line or chasing after a horse who is hightailing it around the pasture, having a grand old time and learning nothing but disobedience.

Tacked up for lungeing. The horse should in no way be restricted by the side reins, but should stretch to the contact.

It's nice to have some assistance for the first session. Have your helper walk beside the horse and guide it for the first few times around. Start off to the left, as most horses go better this way. Position the horse on the outside of a circle with you in the center and urge it forward with the whip and your voice, saying "walk on." Use a firm, sharp voice for the command and have your assistant walk forward with the horse, praising it. After a full circle you should then use a very soothing, drawn-out tone and say "whoooooa," or "ho-o-o," whichever works best. As soon as the horse understands the basic commands, you can dispense with your helper.

It is possible, though difficult, to work without assistance at this stage. If you have no help, keep the line very short so that you can reach your horse with the whip, and follow the same routine as above, saying "walk on," and tapping gently with the whip. It is very important to stay slightly behind the horse's shoulder so you are in a driving position. The biggest problem in getting a green horse to lunge is that it persists in trying to turn in towards you. Staying slightly behind your horse and making it go forward is the only way to prevent turning in. The first session can be difficult; the trick is to keep going until you win and the horse understands.

Twist up the reins and catch them up under the jowl straps of the cavesson.

If you have a nervous horse, you may find it flying away from you in a panic when touched with the whip; this is one reason you need an enclosed space. You must be quite calm, but firm. Touch the horse all over with the whip until it accepts, and finds out that the whip will neither hurt nor go away. It is all important that you persist in this first lesson. It's a basic obedience requirement and part of your domination of the horse. You had better win this one or the horse will soon find out that it need not obey.

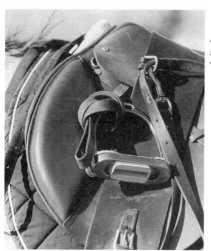

Stirrups tied up to prevent banging on the horse's side. The surcingle with side reins is fastened over the saddle.

The horse needs to be encouraged to trot   *Point the lunge whip at the horse's shoulder*
out freely from the lunge whip.   *to keep it out on the circle. The horse is*
                                                 moving freely forward.

The first stage should pass rapidly, with the horse learning to obey simple commands in two or three days. You can then progress to trot. Since the horse understands "walk on" and "ho," start out in walk and crack the whip saying "ter-rot!" Always stay behind the horse's shoulder so that you are driving forward. Once the horse obeys these commands, both to the left and to the right, you have the basis for serious work.

The lunge line makes it possible for you to develop your horse's balance and rhythm easily without the added weight of the rider. By keeping the horse on a circle, you are developing its ability to bend. Rhythm is all important. You do not want the horse charging around at top speed. It must relax and develop a gait that utilizes the whole body. Many horses move only their legs; they do not use all the other muscles which are so important for correct movement. The quarters must become more active and the horse must stretch its neck and head forward and down so that the muscles along the back come into play. Then, and only then, will the muscles develop and strengthen.

Canter is the most difficult gait for the horse on the lunge line. The confines of the circle are demanding at the beginning of training and you may sharply find that your horse has problems. Just keep insisting that it canter, making a larger circle if necessary, and let the horse find its own balance and rhythm regardless of correct leads. Eventually, you will want the horse to canter circles with you in the saddle, so it is vital that it finds its own balance first. If the horse picks up the wrong lead or cross-canters (leading with one leg in front and the other in back), check quietly with your voice and then urge it forward again. Once I had a young Thoroughbred horse who had never been lunged. The first time I asked him to canter on the circle he fell over eight times. We just kept going and finally he found he could keep his balance after all. But it took the best part of a month before he could canter steadily.

You must be consistent and, above all, patient. Reward the slightest progress so that the horse comes to trust you and understands just what it is that you want. At no stage in training should you neglect work on the lunge. It is invaluable for any horse, no matter how advanced.

Along with the lungeing you should be beginning your mounted flat work. After each day's lungeing session, you should put in at least one half-hour of flat work. This consists of teaching the horse to move under the rider through corners, on large circles and straight ahead, in walk, trot and canter both in the arena and in the open.

It is a mistake to work only in an enclosed ring. You are going to be competing in many places, so why not train in different places as well? If you are teaching something new, it is best to start in an enclosed space or ring as that makes it easier to concentrate on the lesson. Once that lesson is confirmed, you can practice it anywhere.

The first lesson the horse must learn is to *halt and stand* still. That may sound very basic, but how often do you see horses moving around impatiently instead of standing quietly, waiting for their riders' aids? Most dressage tests start and end with a halt, and the horse must stand still.

After lungeing, take off the lungeing equipment, tighten the girth, take the reins, and mount. Check your stirrup length, adjust the reins, attend to anything else that needs adjustment, and insist that the horse stand still, without moving even one foot, while you do this. Then, taking a light contact with your hands, keep your legs in constant contact with the horse's sides and squeeze, giving the aid to move on.

This is the second vital lesson: *the horse must go forward when asked. A* green horse may not be very responsive to the leg aids because it doesn't understand them. It's up to you to explain. If the horse doesn't move forward from a squeeze, don't just kick harder; use the whip just behind the girth in the same place you use your leg. The horse must become as responsive as possible, and the whip is a sharp reminder that you mean business. It doesn't matter if the horse rushes off when you use the whip—which often happens—at least that is some response. The next time you use your leg, the horse should move off at once. If it doesn't, repeat the whole procedure as this is a crucial lesson and one that needs to be enforced from the beginning. If your horse doesn't move forward from your leg, what chance do you have of making it understand what you want?

The rider needs to think carefully about his or her position in the saddle. The legs should lie against the horse and remain in touch at all times. If the lower legs are held away from the horse, each time the rider needs to give an aid they have to be put into contact with the horse's sides. This can surprise the horse and make it tense. If, however, your leg is always in contact, the horse will accept it and will listen when you do use it. On the other hand, if you are banging away at the horse each stride, how can you expect it to differentiate between the banging and an aid when you use one? A quiet leg resting against the horse's side is what you have to work for.

The body should be held erect with the arms hanging quietly at your sides. The elbows should be bent so that the lower arm, hand, and rein make a straight line to the horse's mouth. Your head should be up and you must look where you are going. The stirrups should be fairly long to allow as much leg on the horse as possible. The head, hips, and heels should be aligned.

Having taught the horse to move forward from the leg, the next lesson is to teach it to stop when told. The correct way to stop the horse, or to make any transition to a slower pace, is to use as *little rein as possible* and to stop the horse with *your seat and back.* There are many books that go into great detail on the use of the seat and back. They can be complicated reading. Essentially, the horse must be driven into the rider's hands which will, in effect, "shut the door in front." The rider must sit tall, close the legs, and press the seatbones into the saddle—I find it helpful to ask riders to move their shoulders quickly in a sideways motion. This creates movement in the seat bones which communicates the required effect to the horse's back. This must be done quickly and repeated once or twice, or as many times as it takes to have an effect on the horse. As soon as the horse slows down or stops, pat it and show that this is the correct response. Of course, you are not going to wiggle around like this throughout your riding career, but this exercise does give the correct feeling and has helped countless riders to understand just what is required. It becomes a very refined movement as you progress with your training and, if done correctly from the beginning, it invariably works. The best motto one can adopt when training a horse is *"If it works, use it."*

All the work done at this stage should be "on contact." This means the horse must accept a *light* contact with the bit at all times. As the training progresses, you will find that the horse learns to trust your hand and begins to carry itself. You should not be holding the horse together by sheer force at this point or, for that matter, at any time in your training. The work on the lunge with side reins should teach the horse to accept an elastic contact.

That understanding should carry over to when you are mounted. The whole secret of a light contact comes from the horse's acceptance of your hands and legs. Your legs must be constantly urging the horse forward and encouraging it to step with the hind feet underneath the body so that self-carriage is developed. It won't happen overnight, but there should be a steady progress as the horse relaxes in the back and uses its body more and more correctly.

Gymnastic development of any athlete happens over a long period, but the work must be consistent. For this reason, flat work should be a daily part of the horse's routine through the first year of training. Only by constant work will the correct muscles develop. If you just work your horse one day a week, you will begin at the same point each time. A horse learns by repetition and needs the reinforcement of daily lessons in order to retain knowledge and go on learning.

Dressage means training, pure and simple. A horse doesn't "do" dressage —it walks, trots, and canters. The gaits change and become more educated as training progresses, but for the very basic requirements of the low level tests, all the horse needs to know is how to move forward with an even rhythm and a relaxed attitude, and how to make transitions without any sign of resistance. The horse has to be capable of making circles, bent along the line of the circle, and of having enough balance to move through corners easily and smoothly. What often happens is that riders neglect the basic flat work and then, nervous at the thought of riding a test, they develop "on-the-bit-itis." Don't try to force the horse into a prematurely short frame. You will end up with constriction, stiffness, and resistance. The horse should accept a soft contact with the hands without stiffening in the back or trying to pull the reins out of the rider's hands, and it should move forward from the legs in a relaxed manner. The rider must keep his or her legs on the horse, urging it forward at each step so that there is a feeling of pushing the horse up to the bridle, rather than trying to pull the head and neck back to the rest of the body. The horse must go long and low in front before you start shortening its frame.

Transitions between gaits are important. The horse must have sufficient balance to be able to change from walk to trot and from trot to canter without losing rhythm. It is incorrect for the horse to go faster and faster until it falls into the next gait in self-defense.

A horse is quite capable of taking the canter from the walk, halt, or even rein back, so it stands to reason that a fast trot is not necessary in order to canter. Pay a lot of attention to riding good transitions. Each time you ask your horse to "shift gears" as it were, you are asking it to change its balance.

Frequent changes of gait help make the horse lighter and more responsive.

If you lay down a good foundation in the beginning you will find more advanced movements "falling into your lap" as your training program progresses. But you must be consistent and thorough. Don't be satisfied with a poor transition, repeat it again and again until you get one you are satisfied with. If you are not persistent, you will find all sorts of problems rearing their heads later on.

From a halt, ask for walk. From walk, ask for trot. From trot, ask for canter. Perhaps your horse shoots off in canter; come back to the trot and try again, and again and again, until you merely suggest canter to get a smooth forward transition. For the sluggish horse, use the stick to remind it that your leg means business. For the horse that rushes, stay on a circle and don't ask for very many steps in canter before you come down to trot again. If the horse learns it is going to be asked to trot again almost immediately, it will steady the canter in order to be prepared for the transition down. This may sound fairly simple, but it may take you weeks to achieve. Don't be in a rush, take the time. Be pleased with the slightest amount of improvement, *but don't leave the schooling area until you have achieved some progress.*

Don't expect miracles; expect improvement. Your first sessions may be rough. Many horses have been badly trained and it takes a while to undo the damage that has been done, but with your lungeing and careful schooling, by attempting one thing at a time, you should be able to work your way to meeting the basic dressage standard. Do exercises again and again until you can achieve them with only the slightest hint to your horse. You don't want to have to haul on its mouth or flail away with your legs. Once your horse understands, you will be able to use fewer and fewer aids until you merely "think" the aids to get the results. That is the basis of all your flat work. Riding is supposed to be enjoyable; a schooled horse is supposed to be easy to ride. At first you will have to use a great deal of strength in order to accomplish your goals, but you will find that it takes less and less if you are systematic and persistent.

Start your schooling routine with a lungeing session, which will relax the horse and prepare it for the flat work to follow. Once you mount, plan a logical schooling routine. Halts must be square and motionless, the move-off in walk should be smooth, on contact and active. The transition to trot should be achieved with the horse's head remaining quiet, so that it flows from walk into trot. The trot work should be active and regular, with every step being like the one before. You should be able to work in large circles and make turns across your schooling area so that the horse changes from hand to hand with ease, following an open rein. The horse must learn to bend in both directions, always stepping actively forward with a rhythmic beat.

Uphill work for muscle building and balance.

Downhill work for balance.

When you ride a turn or begin a circle, there should be no change in beat, no loss of rhythm. Learn to push the horse through turns with your legs because if you pull the reins, the horse will lose some of its forward impulse.

With young horses, the canter work under saddle can be put off until you are really happy with the trot work on the flat and the canter on the lunge is balanced and regular. Canter can be done out on cross-country for the first month or so. Often a green horse is not balanced enough to canter circles under the rider. It will depend on each individual horse. If you try cantering and feel that the horse is losing balance in the corners, put cantering off for a while until the overall balance improves.

In addition to flat work, you must be considering other aspects of training, even at this early stage. Your horse must learn to cope with uneven ground and to adjust its balance when going uphill and downhill.

At least three days a week, in addition to the lungeing and flat work, you should be riding out over as many different ground formations as you can find: uphill, downhill, into streams, all at a fairly slow pace, walking most of the time. The more ground you can cover, the better. You'll find that this pays off in your lessons on the flat. By changing the balance when going up and down hills, your horse will improve control over its body in the flat work also. This is a very important part of your training. Later on, you will be tackling uneven ground at greater speeds and your horse must have the confidence and ability to shift its center of gravity. Many show-ring horses are panic-stricken if you try to ride them down steep hills, and it's only because part of their training has been neglected. Even the Lipizzaners spend the first four years of their lives in mountain pastures, galloping over uneven terrain.

The work on hills will also be the beginning of your conditioning program. Building these muscles is necessary in order to negotiate cross-country courses. Your horse should be getting from one and a half to two hours of work a day at this point, six days a week, with one rest day. Your feeding program must be kept current. The more work a horse does, the more feed it requires, so this is an important consideration for the event horse. Giving regular meals, preferably three times a day, allows for better digestion as the horse has a relatively small stomach. Watch your horse's weight carefully, and feed good quality feed, whatever suits your horse best. At this stage, sweet feed is quite adequate when supplemented with good hay. Later on, when you begin serious endurance work, you may find your horse needs to be switched to additional hard feed, such as oats.

The event horse should be stabled most of the time. It will not keep condition satisfactorily out at grass—particularly in the spring. It is important for horses to be turned out each day. Though they don't need a great deal of grass, their attitudes benefit from being out for an hour or two a day. Each horse is an individual and you must study each one separately to discover the correct amount of feed, work, and relaxation to suit it.

3

BEGINNING JUMPING WORK

As soon as your horse is accepting your aids—stopping, walking, trotting, and cantering with a regular contact and making simple turns and circles in an arena—it is time to give some thought to starting the jumping work. There is no better way to teach jumping than to use cavaletti. A set of cavaletti is indispensable to the serious rider. Anyone who can use a hammer and saw can make a set as follows.

The rail should be 10-12 feet in length. Construct the ends by making X's with four-by-fours. When the rail is attached to the ends, you should be able to change the height from 6-8 inches to 12-15 inches or 20-22 inches by rolling the whole structure over. With this type of equipment you can build many different gymnastic formations and you will only be limited by

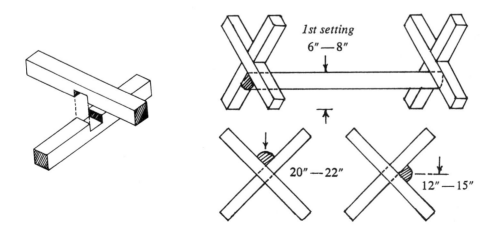

Walking through poles the first time.

the number of cavaletti you build. Six is a bare minimum, with ten to twelve much more practical. You should use rounded poles or bevel off the edges of square ones so that they won't hurt the horse. The rails should be solid. Not only will that encourage the horse to respect them if it raps them, they will also be harder to break.

Some trainers take short cuts and use poles laid on the ground. This can be dangerous as they roll out of place very easily, changing the spacing, and the horse can step on them and twist a fetlock.

Caution: It cannot be stressed enough that *each horse will have a slightly different stride.* Distances given are averages. You must observe your own horse and decide what the correct distances should be. Cavaletti used indiscriminately can do more harm than good. It's a great idea to have a friend help out when you begin cavaletti work. If this is not possible, you must get out to your practice ground and set things up before you get there with your horse.

Your stirrups should be taken up several holes for jumping work. Adjust them before you begin. Jumping requires that you stay in balance with the horse and have a strong base of support for yourself. A neck strap is a good idea with green horses as they tend to be awkward at times and even an

The first time in trot---the horse is not sure how to move its feet.

advanced rider can be hard put to stay with their movements.

Your first step is to put three or four cavaletti, on the lowest setting, around your arena. During the course of your warm-up session, get your horse to step over them, first at the walk, then at the trot, without making much ado about it. Get the horse used to seeing the cavaletti around, and include them in your circles and turns.

The first real lesson is to take the horse through "trotting poles." For this lesson you need five or six cavaletti, set at the lowest height, lined up against the wall or rail, 4-5 feet apart. Most horses will use a four-foot setting for this exercise, but if you have a horse with a very short stride you may need them a bit closer. It is very unusual for a horse to need a longer setting than five feet; that would be an exceptionally long-striding horse. Set another cavaletti at an angle to the first one to act as a guide into the formation.

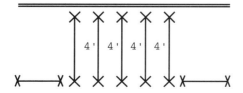

Trotting through in rhythm and balance.

After your warm-up, approach the formation at a walk, looking ahead to the end of the ring. Let the horse put its head down to investigate, but urge it forward with your legs, leaving the reins long. *You* don't have to look at the cavaletti; the horse is the one who has to negotiate them, not you. Repeat this several times until the horse thinks nothing of walking on through.

The horse may stumble—in all probability it will—but just ignore this; it will learn to pick up its feet and respect the cavaletti. This is an important part of the training. Your horse needs lots of encouragement from you, so pat it on the neck and praise it effusively with your voice. If you run into serious resistance, with the horse becoming upset and refusing to go through, ask your assistant to walk through beside the horse with a hand on the rein. After you show the horse that there is nothing to it, the initial fear will evaporate. The main point to put across is that "trotting poles" are certainly not terrifying, and not at all exciting. If you clutch at the reins, dig in the spurs, saying in effect "We're gonna jump! We're gonna jump!" your horse will become tense and learn to rush into fences. If, however, you go about things in a calm, deliberate way, with no excitement, the horse will accept jumping happily and enjoy it. Most of the problems you see in jumping are caused by riders and by the lack of correct fundamental training.

As soon as the horse understands walking through the cavaletti, which should not take very long, you are ready to begin the exercise at the trot. As you approach the cavaletti, ask the horse to go forward in a nice, relaxed trot. It will quickly discover that the cavaletti are spaced comfortably and will trot through with an increased swing to its back. If your horse stumbles or falls, your distances are wrong and should be readjusted before continuing. If you have planned carefully, this should not happen. The whole purpose of cavaletti exercise is to teach the horse to use its head, neck and back correctly to strengthen those muscles for future jumping work. It also instills a very definite rhythm in horse and rider, enabling them to meet fences correctly later on.

The first time through you may have problems. The horse may "die" on you, slowing to a walk since that is what you had asked at first. A horse who reacts this way must be brought in firmly at a vigorous posting trot, with the rider rising and sitting emphatically to keep the forward motion. A little encouragement from the voice and, if necessary, from the stick, will convince the horse to keep the trot. If, on the other hand, your horse rushes through excitedly, taking two or three cavaletti in great leaping bounds, you

Julie Jones

Cantering over poles at a one-stride distance.

Julie Jones

The horse has to figure out how to move its feet.

need to approach at the walk and only ask for a trot as you reach the first one. For a very bad rusher, have your assistant (who must be brave and nimble) stand in the middle of the formation with arms stretched to the side, and ride the horse straight toward him. Very few horses will intentionally run down a person. This remedy has worked countless times, but your assistant must be ready to jump out of the way quickly. Go through the formation straight, otherwise you are not taking advantage of your careful spacing of the cavaletti.

Don't overdo it. Once your horse realizes what is expected and has gone through the cavaletti quietly with good rhythm, quit, make a fuss over the horse, and put it away for the day.

In the next few sessions you can vary the work at the trot, sometimes

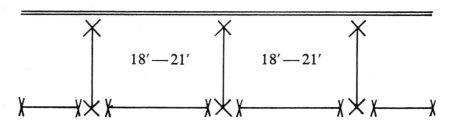

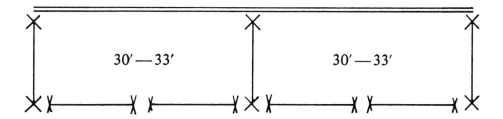

doing exercises to help your own balance. Go through the cavaletti standing up in your stirrups. This will improve both grip and balance. Try going through with your hands on your hips (tying a knot in the reins first). If your work over cavaletti is correct, your horse will be moving in a nice, relaxed rhythm, the neck will be stretched forward and down, and the whole back will be swinging underneath you. Your horse will be learning to trust you and to enjoy the rhythmic exercise. The muscles of the back and neck are being exercised properly, thus being strengthened and developed; the heart and lungs are getting a workout too, and you are learning to move in harmony with your horse.

In the beginning, you might want to work on these exercises every other day for a couple of weeks, varying the placement of the cavaletti in your work area so they are not always in the same place. Don't overdo it. After the horse understands the lesson, you can practice once or twice a week. There is plenty of other work to intersperse with the cavaletti drills.

Once the trot work over cavaletti is firmly established, you can begin work at the canter. This is the first step to real jumping. For canter work you should turn the cavaletti over to the highest setting so that an actual jumping effort is required from the horse. If you canter over the low setting you used for the trot, your horse won't make any real effort and the canter will tend to flatten out—the reverse effect to the one you want. Set out four cavaletti along the fence with a wing or guide into them. This exercise requires that you be very careful about spacing. Horses who have short strides will use a spacing from 18-20'; average horses will require 20-22'; really long-striding horses need 22-24'. The only way to determine the correct distances is to set your cavaletti at about 20' and see how your horse copes with that distance. *The distances between all the cavaletti must be the same.* If your horse seems cramped when it reaches the end of the formation, increase the distances between the cavaletti; if it is really having to reach for them, shorten the distance.

The mechanics of this gymnastic exercise require the horse to jump, take a stride, jump, take a stride, and so on. What you are trying to instill in the

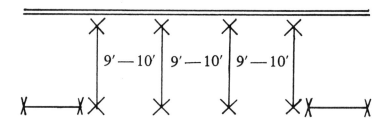

horse is a correct jumping action *in stride* so that later on, when faced with combination jumps, it will understand the effort required and not panic. You are educating your horse logically, not throwing problems at it haphazardly. In addition, you are developing all the correct muscles for jumping. This work is also invaluable for the rider in teaching coordination and the feeling for correct jumping.

Again, approach this new gymnastic at the trot. This gives the horse time to see that something new is ahead, and tends to keep it from rushing, which is important. As you get to the first cavaletti, urge the horse to take the canter and ride firmly on through the formation. The majority of horses will understand by the second or third time through, although the first time may be a bit hectic. If you are having trouble feeling the correct timing, count aloud to yourself as you go through, "One and jump, one and jump, one and jump." After you both have the idea, you can vary the formation by setting distances that make the horse take two strides in between jumps. For this the distance should be between 30' (very short) and 35' (long) with the average probably working out at 33'. A "sticky" horse will use the shorter distances, and you have to find the best one for your horse. Later on you can get much more demanding and ask your horse to do awkward distances, but right now you are trying to do everything in your power to encourage the horse and put it exactly in the right stride to make the exercise simple.

As soon as you are both proficient at these exercises, you can progress on to those which really help develop the proper bascule (arching of the back over the fence). Set three or four cavaletti 9' to 9'6" apart. In this exercise,

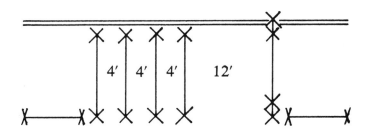

the closer the cavaletti, the harder it is for the horse. With this formation, the horse has no room to take a stride in between jumping efforts but must "bounce" through. This makes the hind legs work very hard and should be used with discretion; four or five times a session is ample. Again, bring the horse in at a trot and let it figure out what to do. Ride firmly forward and be aware that the motion will be very quick so you need to be ready to go with the horse. Grab your neck strap if you are not sure you can stay with the horse. If your horse is sluggish, you can afford to approach this at a canter. The excitable horse should have calmed down by now with the practice at the trot. If not, it is not ready for this new exercise. You'd better go back and do the first steps over. Don't push your horse into jumping or you'll create a real fear. Go back to the early steps *now,* or you run the risk of souring it on jumping for life. All too often riders try to do too much at once and thus create problem horses. Nothing beats sound basic training; it may take a bit longer, but it pays off in the end.

When your horse can negotiate the cavaletti "bounces" straight, calmly and evenly, you can progress on to more advanced gymnastics as a preparation for in-and-outs and combination obstacles. You can change the spacing on your cantering cavaletti between "short" (18') and "long" (up to 26') ones, but use the *same* spacing throughout one line—don't mix long and short strides at this point. Bear in mind that the short strides will make the horse arch its back and the longer ones will make it reach out for a fence.

In addition to all this cavaletti work, you should be continuing the flatwork every day, and you should include some basic cross-country riding in your program. The horse should still be going out and travelling up and down hills. You can include logs, coops, and natural jumps you find out on your rides, and you should go through each and every stream you can find at walk, trot, and canter.

As you progress you will use your cavaletti in other ways. You can combine lungeing work with cavaletti work. Using either cavaletti or poles on the ground set for the trot work, you can guide the horse through a set of five or six poles in a straight line or, even more beneficial, set on an arc.

By placing your cavaletti on the inside of the arc at 4 1/2 to 5 feet apart and the outside at 6 to 7 feet, you can adjust your horse's stride by bringing it close to you in the center of the circle and shortening the stride, or you can move the horse further away from you and make it take a longer stride through the gymnastic. You can also set your cavaletti to the top height for the canter bounce stride on an arc and make the horse bounce through.

Julie Jones

The first step: trotting poles on the ground in a straight line.

The second step: increased lifting and bending of joints over raised poles on the arc of a circle.

Good activity over the gymnastic.

Horse trotting through raised poles, increasing the activity of all four legs and its back.

Cantering bounce poles to increase suppleness and use of the back.

For horses that are reluctant to use themselves, I find that by raising one end of the poles on standards to about 3 feet and placing the other end on the ground, I can make the horse use its joints.

This work comes later on in your training schedule. Remember, it is better to go too slowly than ruin your horse by being overly demanding at first. Teach your horse to trust you and to enjoy the work and your troubles will be minimized.

How is your personal fitness program going?

4

CONDITIONING

Conditioning is an art. It requires a great deal of your time and attention, and can make the difference between an average ride and an excellent one. You must learn to observe your horse and to estimate the amount of stress that it can take without doing damage to its system. "In condition" means that the horse is able to perform the various requirements of the endurance test without difficulty, and without injury.

By the time you start serious conditioning, your horse should be doing one and a half to two hours of work a day, six days a week. *You cannot get a horse into condition in less than two months and, for more advanced competitions, three months should be the minimum.* This includes the preliminary work before you start galloping exercise. The horse who is conditioned slowly and carefully will stay in peak condition much longer than one who is pushed too fast in the early stages.

The preliminary work should be undertaken at the beginning of your yearly riding program. The horse should have been checked by the vet and wormed regularly, as well as having had its teeth checked and all necessary vaccinations given. It is also a good idea to have a blood count taken to make sure there are no internal problems which are not readily visible.

Conditioning means conditioning *the whole horse.* You are concerned with three vital systems: the limbs, the cardio-pulmonary (heart and lung) system, and the skin and muscles. The limbs must be toughened up by putting miles under them; the muscles and tendons must be strengthened and prepared to take great stress without tearing and breaking down; the cardio-pulmonary system must be capable of recovering from exertion. The condition of the skin and of the muscles that lie under it are also important. Dirty skin

Why conditioning? Look at these two photographs. Same horse, same rider the difference is nine months of proper work and conditioning. The top photo is fairly nice relaxed and willing, but neither horse nor rider are very aggressive. The lower photo is very different. The horse is well-muscled, well-developed, and attacking the fence. The rider is well with him and driving for the next fence.

Dewell

cannot breathe nor dissipate heat effectively.

Conditioning begins in the stable. Your horse should be groomed daily. Properly groomed. First the surface mud and dust should be loosened with a rough brush or rubber grooming mitt, then the skin should be cleaned with the body brush (the one with the shorter bristles that reach down under the hair and massage the skin itself). You should finish your grooming routine with a vigorous "strapping" with a stable cloth or wisp. This involves slapping the horse's main surface muscles so that they contract in rhythm with the blows, toning them up and invigorating them by increas-

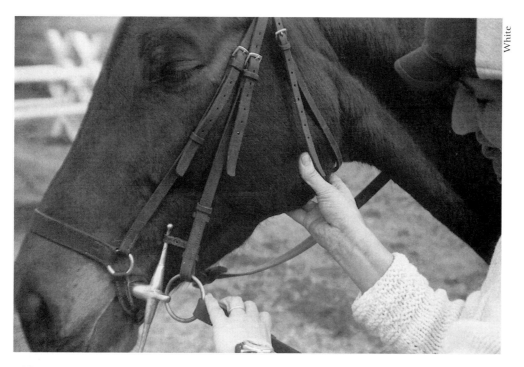

Taking the pulse—eye on stop watch.

ing the blood supply. It works as a thorough massage and can develop muscles in both you and your horse that you didn't even know existed!

The horse should be getting three feeds daily to provide the energy needed. Protein content should be considered. As you increase the work, you will probably have to increase the feed ration. Watch your horse's weight carefully. You don't want it as fat as a show horse; flabby tissue is only excess weight. On the other hand, you don't want your horse looking like a greyhound — all tucked up with the ribs showing, as was the vogue in the past. Knowledge of proper conditioning is more widespread now, and you see horses carrying more weight, but it is solid weight in the form of muscle.

I had a nice mare which I took to a three-day event in Vermont. In the dressage she really blew up, and the dressage judge was scathing. He said "This horse is overfed and under-worked!" This upset me no end. The mare was in really good flesh and absolutely solid muscle all over. The second day, we did the endurance which, in those days, was a real test. The roads and tracks went straight up a mountain for four miles or so, to the start of cross-country. Many horses came in to the ten-minute vet check stressed and were withdrawn. The vet put his stethoscope on my mare, who was hardly blowing, and told me I had the best conditioned horse there. So much for being

The horse must learn to reach out downhill. This is not doing much good because the horse is not coping with its own weight.

Balanced long stride downhill. Rider's stirrups are too long for proper balance.

overweight! A horse doesn't have to be skin-thin to be fit.

If your horse has been in work for six weeks or so, now is the time to start a carefully planned program of conditioning. You should include various exercises to build up the necessary stamina. In the past, riders would trot, canter, and gallop for miles to build up their horses. This resulted in a great many horses becoming damaged from the pounding. With the advent of interval training we have made great steps forward in scientific conditioning. Jack Le Goff, the former USET three-day coach, was a master at the art of conditioning. It is his influence that has revolutionized thinking about conditioning.

What is interval training? It is a system originally developed to train middle- and long-distance runners and is now used extensively by runners and swimmers. Essentially, it is a method whereby the heart, lungs, and muscles are stressed, rested a short while to partially recover, and then stressed again.

The hind leg is well under, but the horse needs to reach out more in front

Horse is attacking a steep slope—this is muscle-building work. Rider's hands are too high.

Julie Jones

Horses need to learn to balance themselves on changes of terrain, up and down.

This builds increased tolerance to stress and can be carefully regulated by built-in checks. That is a brief and very superficial explanation; there are many detailed explanations to be found. The tables for conditioning spell out how to go about it at each stage of the horse's program in detail at the end of each section of this book.

You have to learn to check your horse, so you must know how to take pulse and respiration in order to monitor the progress being made. The pulse can be felt under or between the horse's cheek bone. You can also invest in a stethoscope and place it on the left side of the horse, just by the girth and listen to the heartbeat. You need a watch with a second hand to be accurate. Feel the pulse and count it for 15 seconds, multiply by four, and you have the number of beats per minute. Find the pulse of your horse at rest and make a note of it. Most horses fall between 35-45 beats per minute. Take it several times for an accurate reading.

Respiration can be checked by watching the horse's flank and counting each breath it takes (count only in, not out as well). Again, count for 15 seconds and multiply by four. Alternatively, you can place your hand over one nostril and count each time you feel the horse exhaling. This is sometimes easier. Normal respiration is between 10-15 breaths a minute, but you can run into some odd variations. There is one horse in a local Pony Club which seems to have no normal respiration—he varies wildly at all times of the day, whether in work or in the pasture. But the owner is aware of this and works mainly on the pulse rate. She goes to competitions armed with lots of statistics to back up her claims. The average horse will fall into the normal pattern.

Once you have your horse's normal figures, you are ready to check its fitness. As you work, both pulse and respiration will go up, sometimes quite high. What concerns you, however, is *how quickly they return to normal.* This is known as the *recovery rate,* and is your gauge of how fit your horse is at any time. There are external variables that will affect the numbers; temperature and humidity will make a difference in your readings and must be taken into account.

When you begin conditioning seriously you need a notebook in which to keep a running record so you can adjust your program accordingly. Write down the statistics from your workouts each day and, when you are doing your interval work, keep a record of not only the pulse and respiration, but the weather also.

You must be able to control your program by knowing how far and how fast you are going. Find a large field or track and mark off 400 meters (one quarter mile) or, better yet, 1600 meters (one mile) in 400 meter segments. At the trot, cover 400 meters in exactly 1 minute 42 seconds. It might take you several tries to get the timing correct, but persevere, giving your horse a breather in between go's. This timing means you will be covering the 400 meters at a speed of approximately 225 meters per minute, or nine miles per hour—the speed you will use later on in the roads and tracks. This is a good, on-going trot, perhaps a little faster than your horse normally trots, but most horses can manage it without being terribly pushed.

Next try to cover the same distance, 400 meters, in 1 minute 6 seconds at the canter. This represents a speed of 350 meters per minute, which is the speed normally used at Novice. When you can manage this, the next step up is to be able to cover the same distance in exactly one minute, which is the speed of 400 meters per minute used at the Novice and/or Training Level.

To begin interval work, trot for 5 minutes, walk for 2-3 minutes, repeat this sequence for a total of three 5 minute trots (unless your horse shows signs of distress), then dismount, check the pulse and respiration (PR), walk the horse around for 10 minutes and check again. If the PR numbers stay close to the same after a 10 minute rest, your horse isn't fit enough to start galloping. You will have to stay at this level until you get a better recovery rate.

Presumably your horse has been doing enough work and is prepared for this beginning work and you will find that the PR will return to normal in 10 minutes. Your next step is to try cantering intervals. Young horses and riders should start with a canter of 4 minutes at 350 meters per minute (mpm), walk 2-3 minutes, canter 4 minutes at 350 mpm, walk 2-3 minutes, canter 4 minutes at 350 mpm, then check the PR. If the horse recovers well, you can increase the length of the canters, add a minute to each, so you canter for 5 minutes, even 6 minutes. Any horse that can canter three 4-6 minute intervals can easily cope with Novice, even Training Level courses.

*Hacking

✳ *Never do interval training more than two times a week.* It is as easy to over-train as to undertrain, and you don't want to run your horse into the ground. Preparation for longer courses and faster speeds comes later. If you are just starting out, the work outlined here should get any horse fit for beginning courses. If you do too much speed work your horse will peak too early and drop in condition instead of building up. There is an old saying, "The eye of the master maketh the horse fat"—you can exchange *fat* for *fit*. Learn your horse's reactions inside and out. You have to become part of the horse in competition; study it so that you can become true partners.

You cannot just grab your horse up out of a field and expect it to perform for you. It isn't fair to the horse. Conditioning means the difference between being able to do well and having an unprepared horse. An unfit horse is dangerous. If muscles are not in shape, there is much more danger of falls and/or injury to you or the horse. It's like anything else—if it's worth doing, it's worth doing well.

5

MORE JUMPING AND CROSS COUNTRY WORK

In addition to your dressage work, your conditioning program, and your feeding and grooming routines, you must work on your horse's cross country education. By now you will have been using the basic gymnastics outlined earlier in the section on cavaletti work, and your horse should have developed a certain amount of natural rhythm and balance. The muscles necessary for jumping are steadily developing. Your horse should be jumping little fallen trees and logs out on hacks. Now is the time to start confronting the types of obstacles that you can expect to find on cross country courses.

A word about position is in order at this point. Many people tend to ride over fences with their stirrups much too long. Keeping your balance and staying in balance with the horse is difficult enough. If your stirrups are too long your leg will be weak, you will have no base of support, and you will tend to move around on the horse's back, upsetting its balance. If you shorten your stirrups sufficiently, you create a firm base of support with your lower leg against the horse, and you will have created built-in "shock absorbers" to help take up the jar of landing from a fence. Think of the joints of your leg that are involved: ankle, knee and hip. These joints act as compressed springs to handle your weight. You wouldn't think of jumping off a six-foot wall and landing with your legs straight, would you? If you did, the shock would reverberate right up through the top of your head. You would bend your knees and hips on landing to absorb the shock. The same holds true of jumping; your "shock absorbers" have to compensate for both

The classic position—strong, balanced, head up, eyes fixed ahead.

the momentum of the horse and the jar of landing so that you can maintain your equilibrium. Without balance, you have no way to control your horse's balance and rhythm.

Your basic position will remain much the same as it is for dressage, which is to say that your heel, hip, and head should be on one line. The difference in jumping is that the leg will be bent to a much greater degree to give you added support, and the upper body will be in front of the vertical to keep you over the horse's center of gravity. A common mistake that many riders make is to grip very tightly with the knees while letting the lower legs swing backwards and forwards. This gives little real support, only a pivot point. A close contact with the lower leg is important because your calf and heel must be in contact—both to urge the horse on and to give you that essential solid base. There should be no daylight between your lower legs and the horse's sides.

When you are furthering your horse's education, you must be sure to make jumping as easy and enjoyable for it as you can. You must know what is easy and what is hard for the horse. There are four basic types of obstacles: upright fences with all the lines of the fence in a vertical plane; spread or ascending fences that slope from the lowest part to the highest; square

Strong driving position—head up and eyes focused ahead.

Julie Jones

fences, or oxers, with the front rail and back rail at the same height and spread; and fences without height, such as water or ditches. The easiest of these are spread fences. This is because the horse can easily judge both height and width. The most difficult is the vertical (straight up-and-down) fence.

You can set up various types of jumps in the schooling area where you have been working over the cavaletti formations. Initially, none of them needs to be very high and if you set up a vertical, it is a good practice to use a couple of poles crossed in front of it to give the horse a chance to judge the take-off better. In the beginning, none of the fences should be much over 2'6" to 2'9". It isn't how *high* your horse can jump that matters at this point, but *how* it jumps. Be sure that all fences are solid and inviting. Flimsy wooden rails are not easy for the horse to see and can cause refusals. Make your jumps as solid as you can by using fillers of one kind or another; rails, logs, barrels, and railroad ties (if you can get them) all make ideal schooling material. You should vary your jumps as much as possible to accustom your horse to taking any odd-looking obstacle without hesitation. The worst jump you can put up is a single thin rail with nothing under it.

Start the schooling session with a few goes through your trotting and catering cavaletti formations. This routine has the advantage of limbering the horse up and letting it know what is expected. You don't want to go out cold and jump single fences. When your horse is warmed up and moving with good rhythm through the various gymnastics, you can then prepare to jump some other fences.

In the beginning, it helps tremendously to place a cavaletti one full stride away from the fence. Depending upon your horse's stride, which you are familiar with because of your practice with the cavaletti, you should set the "guide" at a distance of 18-22 feet away from the actual fence. As you make your approach at the trot, your horse should pop over the cavaletti, or "guide," and be in the correct spot to take one more stride before the fence. This makes it easy for the horse and there should be no problem whatsoever.

The first few times you try this, make sure that the fence is inviting and set it either along the side of the arena or between two good, solid wings. This will discourage run-outs. The fence should be solid and sloping with a definite ground line. The whole secret to teaching a horse to jump and enjoy jumping is to present it at fences which are easy and inviting. *Above all, do not overdo it.* Make it as easy as possible for the horse to jump correctly and be sure to reward generously afterwards by patting and praising.

As soon as your horse will take several different single fences calmly and quietly without speeding up, losing rhythm, getting upset, or "wobbling" into the fences, you can arrange three or four in a sequence. Here again you must be sure that there is plenty of room between fences. Continue to use a guide in front. The importance of the guide is to ensure that you and the horse make a correct approach to the fence. Ninety percent of the mistakes in jumping are caused by the rider making a bad approach. If you plan so that the horse is put into the correct stride, it will learn to be calm and confident.

Later on there will be times when you make a mistake coming into a fence and you will have to rely on your horse to get you out of trouble. If you schooled it right, the horse will develop what is known as a "fifth leg" so that it can think for itself and get out of difficulty in spite of you. Do teach your horse to think for itself—don't try to do everything yourself. Both of you have to learn to trust one another, and first experiences are very important. Don't over-ride—let the horse work things out for itself.

If you have been logical and thorough in your preparation with the cavaletti work, you should be able to negotiate a simple course of eight to ten fences in very little time. Again, remember that it isn't the height of the

Walking through a stream for the first time—the horse hesitates.

Now the horse has the idea—cantering through.

jumps that matters at this point; it's the correct approach, the ease of execution, and the style that count. You want to teach your horse to keep a steady pace, making smooth, easy turns in balance, and to enjoy the jumping experience. All too often, riders themselves become tensed because they are going to jump, and the horses feel the tension and get equally excited. Think of riding a course of jumps as riding a set line through the arena at a steady canter. Incidental to the line are the jumps. Think of each fence as just another cantering stride. If you ride the line, instead of each single fence, you will find that the course will take care of itself.

Once your horse understands basic jumping techniques, it is time to move out into the open and begin the work which will lead to riding cross-country courses. You should have been working both uphill and downhill. Right from the very beginning you should ride through any and all streams you can find. If your horse is reluctant to go through water, spend an afternoon, preferably with another experienced horse along to give a lead, doing nothing but walking, trotting, and, eventually, cantering through as much water

First time approach—the horse is not certain he wants to do this.

Don't let the horse turn away.

Show the horse the way with a more experienced "buddy."

The "buddy" gives the horse confidence.

as you can find. It is only fear of the unknown that causes horses to balk. Start out with a narrow stream with a good bottom. Don't try to start out in deep mud. Walk your horse through several times from each direction. If it balks, just keep urging forward with a firm leg, tapping with the stick if necessary. Have the other horse ride off into the distance so that your horse thinks it is going to be abandoned. Make a big fuss as soon as the horse walks through and continue to walk back and forth through the water for as long as it takes until the horse does it matter-of-factly. Then trot and canter through. You can dispel your horse's fears in one session if you persist and it will pay off handsomely in the future.

If you can find a stream that has a little log either in front of it or in the middle, so much the better. After the horse goes through plain water, start working on jumps into water, out of water, and in the middle of water. At the Novice level you should not have to face any water jumps. As long as your horse has been taught to go through water as a matter of course, you should not have any trouble with cross-country fences involving water. Real

Allow the horse to walk around in the water with the company of other horses.

Repeat the walk sequence several times.

Once in the water, pat the horse and let him walk through so he's no longer apprehensive.

Then the horse learns to trot through.

splash fences come a bit later, at the Training Level.

You should, however, introduce your horse to banks, drops, and ditches before you go for your first event. Find a simple drop to start on. The horse should be ridden firmly up to the edge and urged to drop quietly down. Many horses will want to stop on the brink and look. Don't look down yourself—look forward to where you want to go. Your job is to sit tight and urge it on firmly with the leg, voice, and, if necessary, some light taps with the bat. *Don't go out to teach your horse anything without a bat*—that's asking for trouble. For dressage, a long whip you can use without taking your hand off the rein is correct, but for jumping you need a short, firm bat that will give a loud "Whap!" when used.

Starting with a little drop makes it possible for your horse to go off the edge from a standstill, so you must *never turn away* once you have started. Stay there as long as necessary until the horse drops down. When it does, praise and reward by giving the rein and patting effusively, and then go back *right away* and do it again and again until the horse thinks nothing of it. Just

This fellow is now confident enough to canter in.

Follow the leader up and down a simple bank formation.

A simple drop.

Rider and horse looking down into a simple ditch, resulting in a refusal.

getting down once is not enough. Repeat the lesson until it is confirmed in the horse's mind.

Whatever you do, don't tackle a drop of more than two feet the first time. You can really scare the horse by demanding too much at the beginning, and cause problems for the future. As soon as the horse has confidence, you can gradually increase your demands until it thinks nothing of dropping over five feet calmly. *Warning: don't practice drops very often.* They place a good deal of strain on the front legs and can cause injuries. Once your horse has the hang of it, try to take only one or two in a session and then quit.

Another frequent stumbling block on cross country courses is the ditch. There is no excuse for a horse to refuse a ditch. The fault lies in lack of preparation on the part of the rider. Again, be content with small beginnings. Teach your horse to jump little ditches with confidence, and the bigger ones will cause no problems.

Begin with a ditch that is not more than three feet wide and very shallow; the depth of a ditch is more frightening to a horse than the width. It is nice to have an experienced horse along the first time you school over ditches.

On the second try, they are more focused forwards.

A young horse launching over the basic ditch.

The first jump up onto a bank.

Julie Jones

The horse has taken off too far away, leaving the rider behind the movement. Lean more forward while jumping onto a bank.

Nothing gives a horse more confidence than seeing another one going on in front.

Have your "leader" trot over the ditch, then ride your horse energetically forward, close behind. With any luck, your horse will follow the lead and pop on over. Then try again by yourself. If your horse stops, *don't turn away*—urge forward, use the bat, and keep your hands well forward. *Don't look down, look forward.* Your horse can jump up to six or seven feet from a standstill, so don't allow it to turn from the ditch once you are there. Perhaps the horse will put its nose right down to sniff the ditch. This is fine and usually comes just the instant before it makes up its mind to go. When the horse decides to go it will probably be with a great lurch forward, leaving you in the back seat. Be ready for this—grab the mane or, better, the neck strap you have so thoughtfully provided yourself with, so that you don't interfere with the mouth. Green horses often jump awkwardly. Once you have the horse over, praise, and repeat the whole exercise again and

Julie Jones

This horse is also a little too far back on the take off.

Larry White

Up a small bank. This rider is a little too far forward.

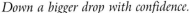

Down a bigger drop with confidence.   *Dropping down three steps in balance.*

again until there is absolutely no hesitation whatsoever. Proceed at once to a slightly larger ditch. You might as well establish this important lesson by showing the horse that ditches are child's play.

If you spend two or three days on this type of schooling, your horse should be fully confident when facing any type of fence that includes a ditch. You are not going to go out and jump Olympic-size ditches right away, but your preliminary work will have laid the foundation for the big fences of the future. Never forget the reward and the praise; they build up the horse's self-confidence and make it willing to tackle unfamiliar obstacles when asked.

Your horse must also learn to jump up onto banks as well as down drops. Find a small bank you can pop onto and then off again, or jump back up the small drop you have just come down. Most horses will jump up onto a bank more readily than they will jump down. All you have to do is to ride firmly forward and try to take off fairly close. A horse that takes off too far away runs the risk later of bellying-out at big banks and catching the stifle joint on the take-off side. At the Novice level this seldom, if ever, happens because the banks are not big enough. You should try to find an Irish bank that requires your horse to jump up, take a stride, and jump down again. This combines the two actions: jumping on and jumping down; lean forward to jump up, and lean backwards and slip the reins to jump down. You must keep a firm leg on while jumping up, as the horse must reorganize its feet to jump down again. Take it fairly slowly at the beginning to give the horse time to coordinate its movements.

All these training sessions can take place over a period of four to five weeks. Tackle one kind of fence at a time. Don't throw everything at the horse at once. Remember, the horse has a small brain—one lesson at a time is quite enough. They have phenomenal memories and a bad experience at this stage can catch up with you and haunt you at some later date in competition. Be sure that you do all the ground work both logically and thoroughly. Such a training program will stand you in good stead later.

Cross country work once a week and stadium work once a week is all the jumping a horse needs. Over-jumping leads to injury and soreness. The horse will sour and grow to dislike the whole idea of jumping if you keep hammering at it. Be sure to continue your lessons, but don't drill incessantly.

6

PREPARING FOR COMPETITION

When you have been following your training program for about four months, it is time to start thinking about your first competition. You and your horse may not be quite ready yet, but in another month or two you should be planning to enter a Novice level horse trial.

There are several important things that you must do that do not involve your horse. First of all, you must find a copy of the current rule book and study the rules. You'd be surprised at the number of first-time competitors who have only a hazy idea of the rules, and they are often eliminated because of some simple infraction stemming from the lack of knowledge. *Read the rules* and ask questions about those that are not quite clear to you. For information about the organizations governing the sport, see Table 2.

When you get your rulebook, study it carefully , especially the parts that apply to the actual riding phases. You don't have to be familiar with the organizer's end of things as yet, although it wouldn't hurt to read that through as well. Look at the pictures of the dressage arenas and think about finding a place to practice so that you and your horse become familiar with the boards and letters. Believe it or not, I have judged at competitions where a competitor has told me that it was the first time the horse or rider had ever been in a proper dressage arena. The end result of this lack of planning was that the horse shied at every marker all around the ring, and the whole test was a disaster from beginning to end. Borrow the motto from the Boy Scouts, "Be Prepared."

Read the rules covering the jumping phases. Learn about the starting box, the requirements of saddlery, etc. There is no point in being eliminated simply because you haven't bothered to find out what the rules and regulations are. Now that you have a rule book, you will see that the Beginner Novice, or whatever the local organizer happens to call the division for beginning riders, requires you to ride a specific dressage test. Get a copy of that test.

Your dressage ride will be essentially walk, trot, and canter each way in the arena, with transitions between the three gaits. If you have never ridden in a dressage show, you should take the time to find out if there are any schooling shows nearby. There are many dressage organizations around the country—contact your local club and find out how you can enter a schooling show. This will give you the chance to ride under competition conditions and will help your horse become accustomed to a proper show.

Riding in a schooling show gives you the opportunity to concentrate on the dressage phase. It may well be that your horse will need such exposure three or four times before it accepts the strange surroundings quietly. Take the time to do this now; you will both learn a great deal. Don't be afraid to ask questions. No one will laugh at you; that's the idea of schooling shows— they are meant to be learning experiences. Read your test sheet over and, if you have questions, the judge will probably be glad to discuss them at the end of the competition, time allowing. Your horse's weak points will show up in the marks and you will know what it is you must work on for the future.

Included in your training program should be some appearances at local hunter-jumper shows. Just as your horse has to get used to performing in the dressage arena, it must also learn to jump strange fences in show rings. The local hunter schooling shows are ideal for this as the courses tend to be very straightforward and simple. Enter the Baby Green or Green division. You don't have to spend all day at the show; two or three classes per session are quite enough to give your horse a taste of public attention.

Schooling for cross-country has to take place at home or at neighboring establishments. Most farms that have courses are willing to let people school for a small fee provided an event is not coming up in the near future. Again, if you really look for schooling facilities you can usually find them. Beginner Novice courses are simple, so your horse should be in good shape if it jumps regular coops, line fences, timber in the form of big logs, and, of course, the little ditches, drops, and banks discussed earlier. Whenever you ride out on your conditioning hacks, look for things to jump. There are plenty of opportunities if you keep your eyes open.

Make sure that you can meet the entry requirements for an event. First, you have to decide which event you want to enter. The USCTA can help here by sending you their Omnibus schedule which lists all recognized events. Your Area Chairman will probably know of smaller local events that are not recognized. These will probably offer the beginning levels. (A list of the Area Chairmen can be obtained from the USCTA.) When you get your entry blank, notice that events, like dressage shows, *require* preregistration. You don't just show up on the day to enter. The time schedules have to be carefully worked out, so the organizer must have your entry early. Check the veterinary documentation requirements for your state. Some states require more certificates than others, and required tests may have to have been done within six months. Make sure all necessary tests are up-to-date.

Then, two weeks to ten days before the event, have your blacksmith either reshoe your horse or check its shoes. Don't leave this to the last minute; blacksmiths are busy people and you may find that if your horse loses a shoe, you will not be able to get it replaced in time.

Check all your equipment carefully for loose or torn stitching. It is extremely dangerous to have the stitches on your girth part company just as you take a fence. All the equipment for eventing is listed at the end of each section—copy it and check off each item as it is packed into your trunk.

Your horse should be properly trimmed, the mane and tail pulled evenly. Again, these are things that should be done over a period of two weeks or so, not at the last minute. Check to be sure you have a copy of the correct dressage test, and memorize it. All tests in Combined Training competitions must be ridden from memory.

Find out how long it will take to get to the show grounds. If it is more than an hour and a half drive, you should consider stabling overnight at the event. A two hour drive to get there, competing all day, and a two hour drive home makes for a very tired horse and rider.

One of the most important things is to find help. Eventing is strenuous and there are so many things to do at an actual competition that it is well nigh impossible to cope by yourself. Get a friend to go with you to help with the care of the horse, and the work of getting ready. It makes life a lot simpler. Good help can make the difference between enjoying an event and going home totally exhausted.

7

THE FIRST COMPETITION

In deciding on your first outing into the competition world it is a good idea to check with someone knowledgeable about the sport. *Not all courses at the beginning levels are comparable.* They can vary widely, and you would do well to take the advice of someone with experience so that you don't go to an event only to find a substandard course that might destroy your horse's carefully built-up confidence. Take the time to do some checking before you enter. Ideally, a Novice course should offer solid, imaginative obstacles that invite the horse to jump boldly. Avoid any course that seems trappy with flimsy, poorly constructed fences. A Novice course should be such that the majority of the horses complete it without faults.

Figure out how long it will take you to get to the show grounds. It is important to remember that you must allow exactly the right amount of time for your warm-up. Don't rush yourself. If you aren't sure just how long it will take to get there, make a dry run, and then add the extra time it will take pulling a trailer. If the event is more than an hour and a half away, take your horse the day before.

Set your alarm early if you are driving to the event on the same day. Allow at least an extra half hour for unforeseen delays—car won't start, flat tire, horse won't load, can't find your coat, etc. You can find out your starting time the day before by asking the secretary of the event during the official cross country walking. That way you know exactly what time you are to enter the dressage ring. Start planning your timetable to allow the correct amount of time to get you to the ring in good shape and ready to go without hurrying.

Larry White

The horse is braided and clean, ready to compete.

Consider your warm-up time: how long does your horse take to settle down and go best? 15 minutes? Half an hour? Does it need to be lunged first to settle down before you ride? Allow enough time to get your horse in the best possible frame of mind for the test. Events generally run on time so you can do your planning exactly.

Allow time to arrive, get your horse out of the trailer, brush it off, tack up, and get yourself dressed. Add this to the time it takes to get there. Then add the time it takes you to feed and braid before leaving. Some people braid the night before; this is fine as long as you don't have a horse who rubs the braids out overnight. Braids always look tidier if they are freshly put in. If you are wise, you have checked your list for the horse and yourself and packed the car and trailer the night before (except for last minute items, see the equipment list).

By all means use a check list. The rush of getting ready to go generally means that some vital piece of equipment will be left behind. Competitors often go through a phase of leaving something different every time; once we forgot a martingale, once a girth, once a pair of breeches (that was the time my eldest son had to borrow a pair from a girl in order to make it into the ring on time). Check each item carefully before you load it all.

Both you and your horse should be turned out immaculately. It is a tribute to your horse to have it looking its very best. Tack should be spotless, the horse trimmed and neat, mane braided and tail pulled. You should be neat, workmanlike and looking your best. Put on your white breeches, stock, and boots before you warm up; leave your coat and hat until you are almost ready to enter. I find it really difficult to keep clean in white breeches, so I use a grooming apron or cover-alls until the time I am due in the ring. I lunge and warm up with protective clothing so that I can keep clean. This is one of the times your all-important helper gets into the act; you need someone to help you tidy up before you go in.

DRESSAGE TEST

After you have warmed up and it is nearly time to go, wipe the horse over with a stable cloth, take off the tail bandage, put on hoof dressing, and check the girth. Put on your coat, straighten up your stock, make sure you have a hair net if you have long hair, put your hat on straight (not tipped to the back of your head), and don't forget your gloves. Just before you go in the ring, have your helper wipe off your boots.

Before you actually enter the ring, ride around the outside of it a couple of times after the horse in front of you has finished. Let your horse see the trailer or umbrella and table where the judge is sitting, as well as the pots of flowers or other markers around the ring. Take the time to ride back and forth in front of the judge; then your horse won't spook coming up the center line. Someone will check your bit (and spurs, if you wear them) to make sure it is legal.

When the whistle blows, or bell rings, get lined up with the center line, *drop your whip* if you still have it, and, as a final touch, *smile* as you trot smartly up the center line towards the judge. The judge's first impression of you and your horse can influence the first mark. Give the judge the impres-

Warming up in casual attire, with bandages. The horse is relaxed and attentive.

A grooming apron helps keep clean.

Tidy and ready for entry. Smile!

Ride around the arena past the judge's stand and the flowers.

sion that you are relaxed and happy and know just what you are doing and that you are inordinately proud of your horse. A big smile never hurts. So many times people look terribly grim and as if they are about to burst into tears in the ring. You may feel like that, but don't let on. Even if you are having problems, grin and bear it.

Make your salute sharp and snappy. Don't do a long, slow lean as if you are falling off the side of your horse; sit up straight. A female drops her right hand to the side and bows her head, not the whole body, then puts the hand back on the rein and trots forward. A male takes his hat off with the right hand, brings it smartly to the side, keeping eye contact with the judge (not bowing), puts the hat back on, gives it a tap to make sure it is secure, puts the hand back on the rein and moves forward. If you are using your helmet with a chin strap, you can give the same salute as a woman: drop one hand, nod your head, then proceed. Judges see a lot of variations on salutes, none of them correct. Don't wave at the judge like an old friend; make it smart and businesslike.

The horse should stand still and square on all four feet; however, if it fidgets and refuses to stand still, get your salute over and done with and move on to the next part of the test. Don't stay in the middle of the ring trying to fix the halt. The judge has already noticed your problems and there is no sense in compounding them—move off with the resolve to get excellent marks in the rest of the test.

Move straight forward and, if you are going to turn right at C, position your horse to the right in preparation for the turn. Get your horse moving forward in a regular rhythm in the trot. Keep your trot very *regular,* very *forward-going without rushing,* and moving freely. When you change from rising trot to sitting trot, there should be absolutely no difference, no slowing down.

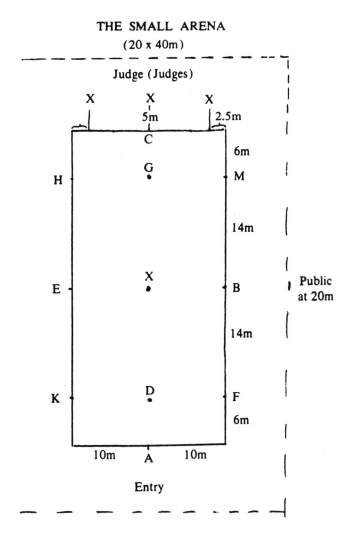

THE SMALL ARENA
(20 x 40m)

Judge (Judges)

Circles at this level are all 20 meters (66 feet) in diameter, which means the width of the dressage arena. A circle is *round,* not *oblong* or *lopsided;* it doesn't have straight sides, it begins and ends at the same point. In a small arena the circle will begin at C or A; touch the track somewhere after the next marker, touch X, touch the opposite track just before the letter, and return to C or A. Caution: in a large arena the circle will be exactly the same *size,* but it will *not* reach down as far as X. Often people riding in a large arena for the first time make a huge oblong because they have been taught to go through X on a 20-meter circle.

When you have a canter depart in these tests, it is perhaps better to ask for the depart a little early, rather than waiting until you get to the letter.

Each movement in a test should be ridden as the rider's body reaches the particular marker, but at the early stages, judges are lenient, preferring to see a smooth-flowing transition a little early than a bad one exactly at the marker. If you can do a perfect one at the right spot, so much the better.

At this basic level, essentially all you do is to show trot and canter each way of the ring and then return up the center line and salute the judge. Be sure to look ahead at all the markers so that you can prepare the horse for the transitions and turns. As you turn up the center line at the end, prepare the turn as you come into the corner preceding it; this way you'll make a nice, flowing turn onto the center line and won't overshoot it because of lack of preparation.

Ride straight up the line again, looking the judge in the eye and smiling your biggest smile. Halt at X, salute smartly and relax your contact on the reins, letting your horse stretch forward and walk out of the ring at A on a loose rein.

That's all there is to it. It really is very simple and nothing to get uptight about. If you have done your homework, schooled your horse to be responsive to simple aids, and taken the time to get a few schooling shows under your belt, the dressage test should be the easiest part of the whole event. It's all in the preparation and homework that you have done. The tests at this level are very easy and straightforward.

After the test, cool out and untack your horse, put it back in the trailer or van, and get yourself ready for the next phase—the crux of the competition—the cross country.

CROSS COUNTRY

Perhaps the most important preparation you will make for your first event is walking and studying the cross country course. It can mean the difference between a successful ride and elimination. Too often novice eventers neglect this important job. I have judged at events where, believe it or not, people have been eliminated and their excuse is, "I didn't walk the cross country course!" That's a very lame excuse. Riding cross-country is hard enough—not knowing where you are going makes it virtually impossible. The more you prepare your plan of attack, the better results you can expect. Mike Plumb, captain of the USET Three-Day Team and many times an Olympian, was once discussing a course before he rode: "I think that it is a difficult course that presents problems. I shall go back and walk it again and again. Each time the fences look a bit smaller—the better prepared I am, the better chance I have of getting around."

You should plan to attend the official walking, which is usually held the day before the actual event. One of the officials at the event will walk

Group walking the course.

around the course with the competitors pointing out any special points such as mandatory flags. By this time you will have a map of the course which you should take along in order to jot down anything you might want to remember later. Now is the time to ask questions about rules. You don't want to make mistakes and get eliminated. *If in doubt, ask.* There are draw-backs to the official walking. All the competitors and their friends are along and sometimes it is difficult to see the fences through the crowd. I know that one of my riders once jumped the wrong fence on a course and it was because he was busy talking to friends and didn't pay careful attention to where the course went. You need to go back and walk it *at least two more times.* First, with your coach or an experienced rider. Concentrate on the course—not only the direction it takes, but each fence as an individual problem. Study the best approach, the turns, the tricky places. You should begin to come up with a good idea of how each fence should be jumped. Jot notes such as "Fence 7, big log, best approach from left-hand side" on your map. Then go back again *by yourself.* This will help to engrave the course on your memory so that when you are riding and the jumps are coming up at you much more quickly than when you were on foot, you will know exactly where you are and what is coming up next.

Some courses are poorly marked. It is often easy to take a wrong turn on wooded portions of a course. Take note of various landmarks and think about the fences in relation to each other. Note the approximate halfway point where you should be checking your time. If you are at all worried about going off-course, take the time to go back again and again until you are sure in your mind. Knowing the course well is half the battle.

In addition to memorizing the course, there are various other things you should think about. First of all, the actual terrain. Is it hilly, wooded, muddy, hard, or good galloping ground? Watch for deep muddy spots. It is all too easy to pull a tendon by going through deep spots too fast. Is the ground hard, and will it become slippery if it rains that night? Decide where you should be cautious and where you can make up time by galloping on. Look for the shortest distance between fences. If there are no mandatory markers, you can take any line you like between two fences. By playing it smart, you can often save yourself a bit of ground and some valuable time.

Consider the layout of the course. Remember that horses are herd animals; they enjoy company. A horse that goes along well in the hunting field may well be reluctant to get out and gallop away from others. The first three fences on course when you are moving away from the other horses must be ridden very firmly, however easy they may look. Any time the course doubles back towards the start or the trailer and stable area, be ready for trouble, as your horse may want to go back to the others.

Most of the fences should be good and solid, much more so than those you may have seen in a show ring. These cross country fences won't fall if you hit them. They may look huge to you, but remember, to the horse they are inviting. If you ride firmly and have done your homework in the schooling sessions, you should have no problems.

Fences that present optical illusions are the ones to be cautious of. An obstacle with a false ground line, such as a bottom rail set in underneath the top one, can make the horse come in too close and catch its knees. Light makes a great difference; look at the fences and try to figure out where the sun will be when you are on course. Any time you have to jump from light into dark (for example, jumping out of a field into the woods), expect the

Irene Cromer

Jumping onto a bank in the woods. The horse has its hind legs well underneath the body.

horse to hesitate. Horse's eyes don't adjust quickly to light changes, and many refusals occur because riders approach this type of fence too quickly, not giving the horse time to adjust its focus.

If there is a lot of clutter on the approach to a fence, or if a fence is jumped towards the trailer area, be sure that your horse is looking at the fence, not at the distractions. Remember too, that horses will jump natural looking obstacles much more readily than they will painted ones. A shiny, newly-painted, white coop, for instance, needs to be ridden just that much more firmly than a plain wooden one. Water fences and ditches seem to cause a great deal of trouble at the novice level, but if you have done your schooling over these obstacles, your horse will accept them without undue hesitation.

Remember that you should never look *down* at any fence. Always be looking *forward*. This is especially true over drop fences. If you look firmly at a fixed point, your horse will feel your determination. Banks and slides should be inspected carefully. They will rarely cause stops, but you must look for rocks or roots sticking up and pick a line to avoid them so your horse doesn't get injured.

The most difficult fences are combinations, though at the Novice level you should not find very complicated ones on your course. If you have an option fence, think out a very careful plan. Decide which way will be best for your horse. Stride out the distances and consider all alternatives. You can't just gallop into a combination and leave the problem up to the horse—if you have come in badly, you may be asking for the impossible. Let's say you have the option of jumping a big spread, bigger than you normally expect at this level, or a simple fence that has a longer approach taking up lots of time, or an in-and-out. If your horse is a big, bold jumper, you could take the spread. If you are at all hesitant about your horse's ability, take the long, slow way. If you don't want to take the bigger fence but feel your horse jumps handily, go for the in-and-out which takes more time, but is not as high. When you have a road crossing where you jump down into a road or path and then go across and jump out again, be very careful. Most horses would rather turn down the road than jump out again.

Don't forget to consider the weather. If you are walking the course the day before the event, make a note of the areas that could deteriorate if it rains. Also make a note of the approximate halfway point so that you can remind yourself to check your watch as you pass it. With the built-in time clock you have developed in your conditioning work, you should have a very good idea of just how fast you are going and whether you are keeping on schedule.

If you ride the dressage test early in the day, you can probably plan to walk the course again *after* your ride. If your dressage time is after 10:00 or 10:30 a.m., you should plan to arrive with enough extra time to take your final walk *before* you ride dressage. Be absolutely certain of the course and go over it in your mind so that you can visualize each fence, and know where each one comes on course. Don't leave it up to chance. Riding cross-country is exciting and you don't want to go out on course and get lost!

Allow time to get your horse tacked up properly, and warm up over the practice fences before you go. Make sure to jump practice fences in the correct direction—as they are flagged for safety reasons. Most people use protective boots for the cross country and it is a good idea to do so. Any horse can take a bad step out on course, and bell boots and galloping boots can prevent injuries. With all the work you are putting into the horse, it stands to reason that you don't want to risk an injury.

Upper-level competitors use different kinds of studs that screw into the shoes for traction. At the lower levels, your blacksmith can help your horse gain more traction by putting small borium "cleats" onto the shoes in front and back. Flat shoes tend to be very slippery and cause the horse to lack confidence.

You need to have the horse's shoes drilled by your farrier so you can add screw-in studs for traction on cross country.

Again, you must have made sure all your tack is in good repair. There's nothing worse than losing a vital piece of equipment over a fence. A safety girth (surcingle) that goes over the regular girth and the saddle can save you from a nasty fall, but it must be fitted correctly, otherwise it can slip back and become an effective bucking strap.

Make sure your own clothing is comfortable and well-fitting and that you have a hat with a harness to keep it in place in case of a fall. A turtle neck sweater with long sleeves can save you from getting scratched by branches in wooded areas. You need a watch that you can read at speed to check your time. *You need spurs and a bat.* Don't think you can ride cross country successfully without either. As Jack Le Goff, former coach of the USET Three-Day Team, once explained; "you wouldn't go to war without a gun." Even the top horses need a sharp tap with the bat once in a while. If you go without a bat and your horse balks, what are you going to do? Reason with it?

About 20 minutes before your starting time, mount up, tighten your girth, and report to the starting steward so he knows that you are ready. Be sure that your number pinney is firmly tied, and that your hair, if it is long, is pulled back out of the way so the jump judges can read your number. If your horse is very excitable, keep your warm-up to a minimum, but trot over the practice fences (in the correct direction) a couple of times to get its muscles loosened up. If you have a phlegmatic horse, get it moving forward smartly and let it know there is work ahead.

Your ride will begin in the starting box. This is a small, roped-off or fenced area. You are required to be in the box and under starter's orders before they count you down. The starter will warn you at two minutes before your time by saying, "Number 15, two minutes!" then again at 1 minute 30 seconds. You don't have to get into the actual box until the last few seconds, and if you have a very excitable horse, it is better to keep walking quietly around outside until the last possible moment. If your horse is really bad, your helper can lead you into the box and wait until you are sent off, to keep the horse quiet. If, on the other hand, you have a nice, calm horse, you can go in and wait quietly for the last 30 seconds or so. Don't jump the gun. The starter will count down, "10, 9, 8, 7, 6, 5, 4, 3, 2, 1, GO!" As the starter says *"GO!"* punch your watch if it is a stop watch, pick up your reins quietly and trot out towards the first fence. You don't have to come out like a shot from a gun.

The first fence must be ridden very firmly no matter how simple because the horse has to realize that you are now on course and that it must leave all its friends. Novice horses often stop at the first fence because the rider doesn't bother to ride it particularly firmly. Ride the whole course as planned, then, after the last fence, ride to the finish flags at a steady canter. Most novice riders seem to think they have to go hell-bent for leather through the finish. It doesn't gain that much time and it may make you stop abruptly, which could cause injury to a ligament or tendon. If you have done a good job of rating your horse cross country, you should be able to finish at a steady, regulated pace. It is unprofessional to do otherwise.

If you do have trouble out on course, don't get flustered. If the horse stops at an unusual fence, turn it around, make a good second approach with a little encouragement from the bat, and deal with the problem. If it should happen that you get eliminated for three refusals, you must then walk your horse off the course being careful not to get in the way of any oncoming horses.

When you come over the finish, pull your horse up in a straight line, gradually reducing the canter to trot, then walk. Halt, jump off, run up your stirrups and loosen your girth. Keep your horse walking for a few minutes before you take the saddle off. Walk back to the trailer, take off the saddle, and then walk your horse around until it stops blowing. If it is a cold day, throw a cooler over the horse's back while you are walking to prevent chills. If it is hot out, the horse will probably cool out faster with nothing on.

Wash your horse off thoroughly with slightly warmed water if the day is chilly or colder water if it is hot. Scrape the sweat off, and walk until the horse is dry. Inspect the legs and feet to see if there have been any injuries and check to make sure you still have all four shoes. Once the horse has stopped blowing and has dried out, it can go back in the trailer until it is time for the stadium jumping.

STADIUM JUMPING

This is the final phase of your first competition. It requires as much planning as the others. All too often competitors get so excited about what happened on the cross-country they tend to forget about the stadium, with disastrous results. Rules have a tendency to change from time to time — one year several new rules went into effect and riders got themselves eliminated unnecessarily because they were not familiar with the regulations. A number of novices, as well as experienced competitors, failed to note that the warm-up fences for stadium, as with cross country, were flagged with red and white flags to be jumped in one direction only. This rule was created for safety's sake to prevent riders from head-on collisions. Ignoring this simple fact has led to the elimination of many competitors.

The stadium phase begins with walking the course just as you walked the cross-country course. You don't just look at a plan of the course and then go in to tackle it. The map of the course should be posted at least one hour before the stadium begins. An announcement will be made when the course is open for walking, and you can walk it any time after that. *Until that announcement is made you are not allowed on the course.* Be sure to check to see which division the course is set for before you walk it. Often different levels jump slightly different courses, so check with an official to see which division will be jumping first. If, for instance, the course is set for Preliminary horses, ask when the Novice riders will have time to walk after the jumps have been reset. There is nothing to stop you from walking the Preliminary course; just be sure you know which jumps your division will be taking. By the time you walk your course the jumps will look a lot smaller.

Walk the course *exactly* as you will ride it. Measure the distances between fences, study the turns carefully, and don't cut corners. Make sure you plan to approach each fence *perfectly straight.* Leave the short cuts and angling fences to the pros; your novice horse needs a straight approach to each fence. Figure out where the sun will be when you jump; stadium often takes place in the late afternoon and the sun can get in your eyes. If you have to jump directly into the sun you should be prepared to cope with the problem.

Pace off the distances in any combination *very carefully.* If a combination is set uphill, remember to allow for the fact that your horse's strides will shorten. If the jumps are set downhill, however, strides will tend to get

The final phase stadium jumping.

longer, and you must be careful to keep your horse from running onto its forehand and flattening out. Look for any badly constructed fences, or fences with false ground lines which, hopefully, won't exist. If you think a fence is flimsy and unfair, you are well within your rights to mention this to the Technical Delegate to see if anything can be done to improve it. Note the position of the start and finish flags—*don't miss them.*

Before you start your stadium round, be sure to check the scoreboard for the official cross country results. You should do this as soon as you hear the announcement, "cross country scores are posted." Be sure your cross country score is correct. Scorers and jump judges can make mistakes. If you think you had a clear round, but are marked down for a refusal, or even elimination, go to the officials, and ask, very politely and calmly, if they will check the sheets. If there is an honest mistake it can be rectified quite easily. However, if you have been eliminated for missing a flag, or some such error, accept the fact and resolve never to do it again. Refusals are sometimes hard to pin-point when you are riding. If your horse came into a drop or ditch and dithered around before jumping, it may well have stepped back without your realizing it and the jump judge will give you a refusal. The ground jury has to rely on the jump judge's word, but riders often feel they know better. Accept the ground jury's decision gracefully. Don't stomp off in tears, muttering "unfair!" All of us have had decisions go against us at one time or another but, on the other hand, all of us have gotten away with a couple of things—so it evens out.

Give yourself plenty of time to get ready for stadium. Check when the jumping will actually begin and try to find out how many horses have to go before you. The average stadium round takes two or three minutes, so if you have 10 horses in front of you, you will go about 30 minutes after your division starts jumping. Check your horse thoroughly before you tack up. Check the legs and feet for any injury you may have missed earlier. Brush off your horse and get yourself tidied up. Get the mud off your boots and tie your stock back on. You will need your coat, hat, and gloves for this final phase.

Take the time to warm up properly. Your horse may be a little stiff after the cross country. Trot and canter a few circles before you start over the practice fences. Jump the fences in the *correct direction.* You are allowed to adjust them to your needs. Start out with a small jump you can trot over to get your horse using its back, then take an upright and a spread two or three times, preferably with a take-off pole in front of the fence. Everyone else will be warming up too, so work with the other riders so you can raise the jumps gradually. Don't try to start off over a 3'3" oxer cold—work up to it logically.

Be sure to check your girth after you have ridden for a few minutes— you don't want to end up on the ground. Watch the ring so that you are ready when the steward calls your number. If the practice area is far from the stadium course, be sure to allow plenty of time to get there. When your turn comes, enter the ring, salute the judge, and wait until the whistle or bell gives the signal to start. If you have done your groundwork, the stadium phase, which lasts two or three minutes, should be relatively easy. You and your horse, being well prepared, should have no problems.

If you do have a refusal, bring your horse around quickly, give it a sharp reminder with the bat, and present it to the fence again. Don't hit your horse going away from a fence—that doesn't make sense. Don't stay in front of a fence for any length of time as this constitutes "showing" your horse the fence, for which you can be eliminated. Don't forget the finish flags. It is heartbreaking to see someone who thinks they have gone clean canter out of the ring in high glee, only to hear that fatal whistle blow.

If you have done well and are in the ribbons, check with the steward to see when the presentations are to be made. If it is at the end of the division, keep your horse close by with the tack on, although if it is chilly, you might want to throw a blanket over its loins. Be ready to ride in and accept your ribbon. It's a courtesy to the organizers.

However, organizers are not always as organized as they should be, and awards can be hectic. If you ride stadium at 2:00 p.m., and they don't get around to presenting the ribbons until after 5:00 p.m., you have a good excuse for putting your horse away so that it can be comfortable.

Remember to return your numbers to the secretary, and leave your trailer or stable area clean and tidy. Organizers go to a great deal of trouble putting on an event and the competitors can make life a little more pleasant if they remember to do their share, smile frequently, and say thank you.

8

REVIEW OF FIRST
YEAR'S WORK

Now that you have participated in your first competition, you must sit down and review the success or failure of your program. Use the competition as a guideline in determining your progress. Honestly now, how did it go? Was your horse upset by the strange surroundings, or did it accept the scene calmly? If your horse was upset, obviously you need to expose it to more strange surroundings. You need to train in as many different places as possible, and to take the horse to more schooling shows so that it learns to work anywhere. A great many competitors use the weather, the muddy footing, the strange place, as excuses for their horse's mistakes. Face it, an event horse must, and frequently does, perform *no matter what.* If your horse never works in the mud and rain at home, it will never go well in mud and rain in competition.

Ledyard '77 was an excellent example of less than perfect conditions. It rained incessantly and the dressage rings were slippery quagmires after the first hour of competition. So who won the dressage? Mike Plumb on Laurenson—and he went at the bottom of the order on the second day, in ankle-deep mud and a persistent downpour. Learn not to make excuses for lack of schooling. *Get out into every kind of weather and work.*

Save all of your dressage tests. However good or bad they were, they offer a valuable means of charting your progress, or lack of it. Read through the comments and see where your performance fell short. That's what you have to work on.

Over a year's showing, your score sheets should reflect definite progress. If they don't, something is wrong and you had better discover what it is. I have sheets that date back into the dim past and they make for amusing reading, but I keep them as a reference. If I run into problems with horses I am working with, I often go back and use the old tests to jog my memory as to what remedies were effective in those cases. Use your tests to discover what the judges are looking for. Judges do vary somewhat, but basically they all want to see the same things, and you will be able to see that from your own tests. If the comments read, "horse not going forward," "lacks impulsion, ... not bent," then you have more homework to do.

How did the cross country go? If you have been following the schooling system outlined, you should have introduced the horse to most of the same types of fences that you would meet on a course. If you did have a stop, consider exactly what happened. Was it your fault or the horse's? Did you lack drive and determination? Did you make a bad approach? Was it a particular type of fence that you have had trouble with before? Had you schooled over similar obstacles before? Did the jump have water or a ditch—the two most common trouble fences?

If you did not do your homework—schooling over a wide variety of obstacles—your horse must be introduced to every imaginable fence which could be on a Novice course and schooled until jumping them is like second nature. Whatever the problem, you must overcome it *now*, not the next time you get into competition.

Was the stadium jumping a problem? It is strange, but riders often spend a great deal of time schooling for cross country and neglect stadium preparations. Eventing involves three separate phases and each has a bearing on the final result. Many top events are lost in the final phase. The New Zealand team was in gold medal position in the Barcelona Olympics, but Spinning Rhombus, ridden by Andrew Nicholson, took down six rails and plummeted them down to bronze. *Don't neglect the stadium and gymnastics schooling.*

Make an honest assessment and then sit down to plan your next moves. If all has gone well, as it should at the lower levels, do two or three Novice events; then give your horse a little vacation. This will be good for it to relax mentally and physically. Try to turn the horse out for at least a month; six weeks is even better. If its feet are good, pull the shoes and give the feet time to grow and expand. Some horses do not have very good quality hoof-walls and cannot go barefoot. If your farrier thinks it is all right, pull the shoes. I had a horse with very bad feet which cracked and never grew good walls. The best thing I ever did for him was to turn him out in sandy soil for five weeks without shoes. The sand acted as an abrasive, wearing the feet down past the poor wall, and encouraged a good, solid growth.

Provided your venture into Novice competition was successful, you will want to move on. If you weren't totally satisfied with the performance of the horse, enter two or three more events to overcome any difficulties. If you have trouble at Novice, there's no point in going on to Training until you resolve your problems. It doesn't get any easier.

TABLE 1: EQUIPMENT LIST

SHIPPING
Shipping boots or bandages and cotton
Tail wrap
Halter and lead shank
Haynet
Sheet or blanket, depending on weather
Lunge line in case of trouble
Broom
Medical kit

STABLE
Feed and hay
Electrolytes, vitamins, etc.
Screw eyes, snaps
Stall guard, if possible
Pitchfork, rake, shovel, broom
Hammer, nails, hooks, knife
Pad of paper, pen, thumbtacks, string
Saddle rack, if available
Blanket rack
Hose
Feed and water buckets
Wash buckets (3 or more—you can never have too many buckets)
Sweat scraper and sponges
Grooming kit: Brushes, rubber mitt or currycomb, hoof pick, hoof dressing, braiding equipment, mane comb, pulling comb, sponge, fly wipe
Sheet, cooler, blanket, rain sheet
Bandages, cotton
Stall card with telephone number where you can be reached
Veterinarian's name and telephone number

TACK
Saddle: one dressage and one jumping *or* one all-purpose
Girths for both saddles and extra, plus an overgirth
Stirrups and leathers for both and extra
Bridles: snaffle, cross country, extra
Breast plate and running martingale, if used
Weight pad (at Intermediate and above only)
Saddle pads, 2 or 3
Lungeing cavesson, side reins, lunge line, lunge whip
Galloping boots, bell boots
Exercise bandages
Tack cleaning kit: sponges, saddle soap, metal polish, leather punch, boot polish and brush, lots of rags

FIRST AID KIT
Alcohol
Antibiotic
Antiseptic wash
Gauze pads and bandages
Cotton: sterile and sheet
Safety pins
Hydrogen Peroxide
Liniment or brace
Bandages: wool, elastic, and track
Bandage pins and tape
Plastic wrap for poultices
Electrolytes
Eye ointment
Colic drench and drench gun
Elastoplast® self-adhering bandage
Spider bandage for knees and hocks
Blunt scissors
(Many riders include emergency butazoladin and tranquilizer
or pain killer, but the veterinarians on duty will have these in supply.)

COMPETITOR'S EQUIPMENT
Coat: black or dark color
Shirts and stock and pin
Cross-country colored turtle neck
Breeches: white for dressage and stadium, other for cross country

Hard hat for dressage
Caliente or helmet for jumping, with safety harness
Dressage whip, jumping bat, spurs
Boots and boot bags
Hard shoes
Work clothes, overalls
Watch and stop watch, tape
Sewing kit
Cooler or thermos for drinks
Chairs or stools
Rain gear
Towels
Gloves: white for dressage, other for jumping
Hairnets

TABLE 2:   THE ORGANIZATIONS GOVERNING EVENTS AND HORSE TRIALS

All of these organizations are involved in combined training in some way, but, as a beginning rider, you are primarily interested in the USCTA (and USPC, if you are a young rider).

The United States Combined Training Association (USCTA), controls competitions and helps organize events all around the country at all levels. The United States is divided into areas. Each area has an area chairman and publishes a calendar of competitions and other activities. The USCTA helps riders and organizers obtain vital information about competitions. A magazine, The USCTA News, is sent to all members. It contains interesting articles and keeps members up to date on rule changes and news from around the country. If you are really serious about the sport, you should become a member. For information, write: USCTA, P.O. Box 2247, Leesburg, VA 22075. The USCTA also has rule books for sale.

The American Horse Shows Association (AHSA) is the American National Federation which represents the United States to the Federation Equestre Internationale (FEI). The AHSA issues rules, licenses judges and officials, and offers annual trophies at various levels. If you join the AHSA you receive a copy of the rule book, published annually, which contains all dressage and combined training rules, as well as a monthly newsletter which updates information in the rule book. Their address is 220 E. 42nd Street, New York, NY 10017.

The United States Dressage Federation (USDF) acts as an educational agency for dressage riders and competitions. They offer awards in dressage competition and sponsor clinics for riders, instructors, and judges. Write to USDF, Box 80668, Lincoln, NE 68501.

The United States Pony Clubs, Inc., (USPC) is for young riders under the age of 21. Pony Club is an educational experience for children, covering all phases of horsemanship. There are four ability "ratings," which are earned by means of testings in riding, stable management, veterinary knowledge, and other areas. Pony Club is primarily eventing oriented, and every year each region holds a "rally" or three-day competition, the winners of which go on to "National Rally" to compete against young riders at their level from across the country. For information, write United States Pony Clubs, Inc., 4071 Iron Works Pike, Lexington Horse Park, Lexington, KY 40511.

The United States Equestrian Team (USET) provides teams for international competition. The USCTA works closely with the USET in providing selection trials for various competitions. The USET headquarters are at Gladstone, NJ 07934.

9

MOVING UP:
THE REQUIREMENTS

What are the requirements for Training Level horse trials? In the dressage phase, the horse is expected to accept the bit, and be able to come "onto" the bit correctly. Lengthening of the stride in trot and canter now become part of the test. Circles need to be more precise and transitions between gaits are more difficult, no longer allowing for intermediate steps of walk. Your dressage schooling will become more intense so that the whole bearing and movement of the horse become more sophisticated. Suppleness and obedience go hand in glove with further training.

Cross country requirements are stepped up, involving greater speeds and bigger fences. Splashes show up on courses, and combinations with more complicated options become the rule. Stadium courses will be bigger and more twisting, with double and triple combinations. Your horse is now out of kindergarten and ready to go into first grade. You will have to set up a curriculum that will enable it to meet these increased demands.

At the beginning of the year, map out a plan for your competitive season. Depending upon where you live, you will be faced with a spring and a fall season, or perhaps only a summer one. Ideally, your horse went well in the Novice horse trials and you can plan to enter three or four Training Level horse trials as your next step. Make up a calendar like the one in Table 3, marking in the schooling shows, your conditioning program, and the competitions you plan to enter.

Competitions should come in at least three-week intervals, with four being ideal. Don't overdo it. Your horse doesn't need to compete every

Julie Jones

Muscle and energy of the well conditioned event horse.

weekend, even though this is possible in parts of the country where there are many events.

Choose your events carefully. Talk to experienced riders and find out just where the best courses are. Don't spoil all your hard work by asking your horse to jump a substandard, poorly designed course—you could throw a whole year's work out of the window. Course design is improving rapidly, but there are still some courses that are not suitable for inexperienced horses. We cannot all draw up the ideal plan because of the vagaries of competition schedules but, based on the ideal, consider the best way to go about planning the year.

Your conditioning schedule will still be based on interval training, the difference being that you up the speeds and lengths of intervals. At the Training level, conditioning is still not as strenuous as it will be later on for a full scale three-day event, but it is designed along the same lines.

Presuming that you have turned your horse out for a well-earned rest after the previous season, you should bring it in from grass and have it checked by your veterinarian. Have its teeth floated if necessary, worm it, and get all of the necessary vaccinations since you will be traveling around to shows and coming into contact with horses from all over the country. Basic requirements will probably be Eastern and Western Encephalitis, tetanus booster, and flu inoculation, as well as a current Coggins test.

You will also want to start to introduce "hard" feed or grain gradually through the first two weeks until your horse makes the shift from grass to regular feed. Do not give a lot of oats to an unfit horse. That is only asking for trouble.

The first week should be spent walking, briskly and energetically, in the country. Seek hilly terrain as much as possible. Your horse must develop some muscle tone before you start into serious work. Start by walking for 20 minutes a day and increase by five minutes until you are up to an hour and a half. Then start trot work, five minutes the first time, gradually increasing until you can do a 15-minute trot with no effort, and without the horse breaking out into a white lather. This stage should take a couple of weeks, and then you can start on your other schooling—dressage work to limber up the muscles you are producing and make the horse more flexible and responsive, and your gymnastic work with the help of cavaletti.

10
MORE ADVANCED FLATWORK

At the Novice level, all you had to worry about in the dressage ring was that the horse went forward calmly, accepting simple aids at the walk, trot, and canter. Now your horse needs to develop balance, suppleness, and the correct muscles. It is time to think about that overused expression, "on the bit."

"On the bit" seems, at times, to be the most misunderstood expression. It shouldn't be; it is really very simple. The FEI (Federation Equestre Internationale) has a very clear definition: "a horse is said to be 'on the bit' when the hocks are correctly placed, the neck is more or less raised, according to the extension or collection of the pace, the head remains steady in position, the contact with the mouth is light, and no resistance is offered to the rider." Fair enough, let's examine this in some detail.

The first thing mentioned is the hocks. Why? *Because without impulsion from behind you have nothing.* I find that all too often, riders tend to think of "on the bit" as something that happens from the withers forward. That is the reason we see so many horses with their heads pulled into a false position and their hocks trailing behind. The horse must learn to step underneath itself so that the hind legs carry more and more of the load, freeing and lightening the forehand. As the horse reaches forward with its hind legs, it will drop its head to receive the contact with the rein, giving an appearance of roundness and balance. Think of the horse as a spring. You are going to compress that spring by driving one end of it forward with your legs and you will receive the energy thus created in your hand. If you merely drive

Acceptable frame for the Novice level. The horse is relaxed, but the rider must ask for more forward movement.

forward and let the energy escape out the front, you will achieve little. If, on the other hand, you pull the front of the spring in but do nothing with the back end, again, you will achieve nothing. You must balance the horse from the back to the front and create a reserve of energy you can then direct in any direction you want. Until the horse is receptive to your legs and hands, you will be unable to lengthen and shorten its frame at will.

There are several exercises which help to bring the horse's hocks underneath it. Riding the horse correctly on circles, which you have been doing, is the basic suppling exercise. When the horse is correctly bent on a circle, the inside hind leg, the one on the inside of your circle, has to be more actively bent than the outside one in order for the horse to carry itself correctly. All too often the rider does not pay sufficient attention to the bend on a circle, negating the whole purpose of the exercise. The horse should be curved on the line of the circle with both hind feet following the same path taken by the front feet. If the horse evades by keeping the hind feet outside the line of the front feet, the circle is not correct. It is helpful to have a mirror to watch yourself in to check this alignment. If that is not possible, get a friend to watch your circles so you can be sure you are riding them correctly. As a last resort, if you have no mirror and no handy friend, ride in a

Going forward on contact, but the head is too high and the back a little hollow. Acceptable at Novice, but not at Training.

circle on a sandy surface and have a look at the footprints. It goes without saying that your circles must be round, otherwise the gymnastic effect of the exercise is lost.

The purpose of dressage exercises is to develop the horse's muscles correctly and evenly on both sides so that it is better able to carry itself and the rider. Pay attention to your school figures and ride them accurately. Dressage movements all have some specific reasons for being; they are based on classical training of the riding horse. Dressage tests are not just a bunch of movements thought up by devious officials for the bewilderment of riders. They have a real and logical application to the training of a horse.

Transitions between gaits reveal the horse's suppleness and obedience. Your horse should flow from one gait into the other as easily as water flows into a stream. A well-known judge once wrote on a dressage test, "Transitions should flow as one river into another. Yours are like Niagara Falls!" Avoid "Niagara Falls." There should be no loss of rhythm or balance as the horse progresses from halt to walk, walk to trot, trot to canter, and back again. Transitions are important, as they show the judge just how correct, or incorrect, your training has been. A smooth transition can only be ridden in balance and rhythm. There is a proper time to ask the horse for a

Larry White

The result of "on-the-bit-itis." The rider is forcing the head down with tight reins and the nose has come behind the vertical. Incorrect at any level, especially Training.

transition in each gait, and the good rider "feels" this moment by instinct and makes it easy for the horse to respond. The horse that is in the correct frame, attentive to the rider, will obey the slightest aids.

From the halt to the walk, the horse should be holding a steady contact on the bit and, when enclosed by the rider's legs, should be ready to move forward. Often riders halt and take their lower leg away from the horse's side. This means they must then put the leg back on before giving an aid. Almost invariably the horse will be startled when the leg goes back on and will stiffen, jerking its head up. The head must remain steady and at the same height through any transition. A slight squeeze with the leg and a softening of the rein contact without letting it go entirely should be enough to indicate to the horse that you want to walk on. If you can't do this with your horse, work at it until you can. Halt to walk is the first transition and you should do it perfectly.

If your horse doesn't pay attention to your leg, it must be taught to do so with a reminder—the whip. The schooling whip is an indispensable part of your training program; you should feel naked without it when schooling. If you have no whip, you have no way to reinforce your leg aids when your

Larry White

Going forward and coming down into the bit. Acceptable at Training Level/First Level. Nose should be in front of the vertical.

horse ignores you. I am certainly not an advocate of beating horses, but I never school without a whip. To those who say their horses are still afraid of a whip and that it is impossible to carry one, I can only say that you must take the time to accustom your horse to it—otherwise your horse is winning the battle.

Start on the ground, rubbing the whip over the entire body of the horse, and progress until you can touch the horse on any part of its body from the saddle. It may take time, but don't let the horse get the better of you by being frightened of the whip. If it has had bad experiences before it came to you, you must do this very vital bit of reschooling if you are to make any progress. The reeducation is up to you. If your horse doesn't respond to your leg, you remind it with a sharp tap of the whip that when you say "go forward" you mean it. In this way you teach your horse to respond to the slightest pressure of your leg. You should never have to resort to constant kicking and pounding with your legs and heels to create forward movement.

It is relatively easy to go from walk to trot, as both are gaits in which the horse moves with a regular two- and four-beat rhythm. The canter presents slightly more difficult problems, being an uneven three-beat gait. There is

Total disaster! The horse is resisting a heavy hand and the rider is not driving forward. The net result is a stiff, hollow, unhappy horse no freedom, no relaxation, and no confidence.

definitely a "right" moment in which to ask for canter. The mechanics of the canter are such that the horse strikes off with the outside hind leg, then places the outside fore and inside hind on the ground together in a diagonal pair, and the final or third beat is made by the inside fore. After this succession of feet there is a brief moment of suspension when all four feet are in the air before the sequence begins again. If you consider this, it stands to reason that the time to ask for the canter is just before the outside hind leg is in a position to propel the weight forward into canter. In walk, the feet touch down as follows: inside fore, outside hind, outside fore, inside hind. As the inside fore reaches forward, the outside hind will be the next support leg; as it swings into place the horse can strike off into canter without doing any rearranging.

In the trot, the legs touch down in diagonal pairs, and when the outside hind and inside fore are about to touch the ground, the horse can again go readily into canter. It all sounds a bit complicated, but think about it and watch your horse's feet when you lunge, then learn to "feel" where they are at all times. Develop the feel for the right moment and your transitions will come easily. In the same way, the transition out of canter is easiest for the

If the horse does not halt squarely, use the whip as a reminder.

horse when it reaches the moment of suspension. Then it can rearrange its feet into a new pattern as it comes down. The third beat of the canter comes as the inside (leading) fore leg hits the ground. This is the time for the aid. When you advance to flying changes, you will use the same timing for the aid to change so that the horse can rearrange its legs and come down in the new lead. If you want canter to trot, canter to walk, or even halt, ask at the correct moment and you will be surprised how much easier it is to obtain the desired result.

As training progresses, your horse should become lighter and lighter to the aids. Once it has learned to move *forward* from your leg pressure, it must then learn to move *away* from the leg. The first lesson for this is the turn on the forehand, a valuable tool in teaching the horse to move from first one leg and then the other, and a tool you can discard as soon as it has served its purpose and the horse understands what is expected. I see no value in practicing the turn on the forehand once the horse has learned the lesson.

Halt near the fence or a wall and turn your horse's head very, very slightly towards the outside. If you are facing to the left, turn your horse's head so that you can just see the arch above the eye on the right side, keeping contact with your left rein so that the horse doesn't turn the head too far.

Irene Cromer

The aids are harsh so the horse has stiffened and the reins are restricting the movement.

Then place your right leg behind the girth (your whole leg from the thigh down, not just your heel) and push gently so that the horse takes its hindquarters away from the wall towards the middle of the arena. Using the wall or fence prevents the horse from stepping forward.

Ideally, you want the horse to cross its right hind foot over in front of the left hind leg until you have completed a 180 degree turn and are facing to the right. Walk forward, then repeat the exercise until your horse moves easily and rhythmically around the turn. Be sure to work equally on the other hand, that is, facing right, turn to the left. You have now taught your horse the very first lateral movement.

The second lateral movement you should teach is leg-yielding. In leg-yielding the aim is to get the horse to move forward and sideways from the

Irene Cromer

*More correct leg-yielding.
The horse moves easily
away form the leg, with
a soft contact on the rein.*

rider's legs. As its legs must cross over each other, the horse has to bend its
joints more, which has the effect of simultaneously strengthening and suppling.

Start out at the walk. Ride through a corner on the left rein and then ask
your horse to move away from the fence or wall with your right leg, moving
towards the middle of the arena. Relax the aid and ride straight forward
after a couple of steps, then repeat the exercise until the horse understands
what is required. Again, be sure to do the same thing on the other side. Once
the horse understands at the walk, practice at the trot and keep that forward
impulsion which is so important. Leg-yielding can be practiced almost anywhere: away from the wall and back to it (changing from one side to the
other really helps the horse's balance), across the diagonal of the arena, and

on circles that gradually decrease and increase in size by spiralling in and out with the horse moving laterally.

Don't be overly concerned with the bend at this point. Leg-yielding is only the beginning of lateral work. Most horses will be fairly straight in their bodies or will bend toward your active leg, that is, away from the direction they are moving. At this point it is enough that the horse *moves away from your leg and crosses its own legs over.* This exercise is the basis for such advanced lateral work as shoulder-in and half-pass. It is the beginning of serious suppling work for your horse. Don't overdo it by working until the horse becomes bored; do a little, then do some vigorous moving forward so that you don't lose your impulsion. All lateral work is designed to improve the bending of the joints, making the horse more supple and helping to strengthen the correct muscles. BUT, only if it is done correctly. If you force the horse or frighten or confuse it by asking for more strenuous exercises before it is ready, the muscles will be tense and hard and you can do severe damage. Be sure the horse understands and be content with a *little progress at a time.* A relaxed horse will learn—a tense, confused horse will fight.

There's more to dressage than going sideways. Now that your horse is in "first grade" it has to develop the beginning of extensions. Lengthening at the trot and canter should be included in your work. Once the horse is on the bit, accepting the rein and stepping under, with the hind feet tracking up in the footprints of the front feet, you can begin to teach it to lengthen and shorten its frame and stride. Loosen up with your routine work at the trot, then ask for a few strides of a longer trot. Ask the horse for more energy. From a very energetic circle, ask the horse to go either straight down the side of the arena or across the diagonal. In rising trot, ask more with the lower leg, at the same time lowering the hands slightly to offer a greater length of rein. Don't throw away the contact, but offer the horse a chance to lower its head and neck. Be content with very slight results at first. After a couple of longer steps, check back, reestablish your working trot, and then ask again for some longer steps. Don't let the horse run away from you by going faster and faster. What you are trying to achieve is a longer, lower frame and a longer stride in the exact same working rhythm. Most novice riders make the mistake of trying to rush into the lengthening. Think of lengthening as looking like a slow-motion film of running to give you the correct idea: long, elevated, slow steps that hover above the ground. That's lengthening.

Until the horse is well-balanced in the working trot, it is hard to get a good lengthening, but you must practice each day until you can obtain it. Your previous work using lots of transitions was the foundation for this work. Now you have to refine your aids so that you can send the horse on

An ideal lengthening of frame and stride.

and bring it back into a shorter frame within the same gait. You are still making transitions, but you are making transitions *within a* gait instead of from gait to gait.

Sometimes it is good to try this exercise on the large circle, sending the horse on for five or six strides and then bringing it back. If you only practice across the diagonal, pretty soon your horse will anticipate, rushing off as you turn across the ring. Remember that the horse must now be responsive to your leg and must learn to reach out when leg pressure is increased, and come back when your seat and back become stronger. A lowering of your seat bones into the saddle and a slight tightening of the thigh should steady the horse. Try to use as little rein as possible—the reins are primarily to position the horse and regulate its frame.

In canter, lengthening is obtained in the same way. On the long side, ask the horse to reach out by increasing your leg pressure and keeping your inside seat bone well forward.

Any lengthening must be followed by a corresponding shortening. In each lengthening there are two transitions: one *into* the lengthening and one *out* of it. Often one sees a rider do a nice lengthening down the side and then go sail-

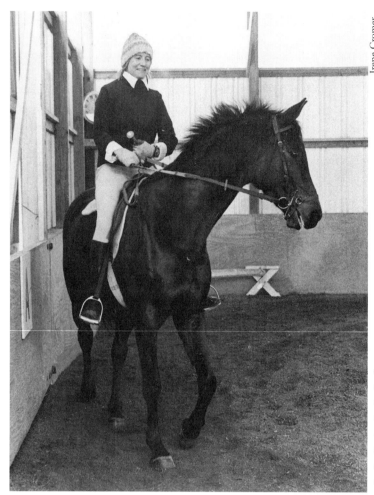

Irene Cromer

A common fault in shoulder-in. A bent head and neck caused by too much inside rein, the rider's inside hand has actually crossed over the withers.

ing around the short end of the arena still in the same frame. You must be able to play your horse like an accordion, in and out, longer and shorter. Later on, in jumping combinations, this flat work will pay off handsomely. Lengthening is not correct unless the horse *lengthens its entire frame and body as well as the length of the strides.* A horse with its head stuck up in the air and a hollow back can never achieve a true extension. Everything must lengthen. This work takes time, but it is all part of the horse's continuing education.

The way to suppleness is through the lateral movements. Once your horse has the basic idea of moving away from the leg (leg-yielding), you can go on to shoulder-in, half-pass, and haunches-in. With these movements, don't expect to be perfect the first time; your horse has to learn the requirements

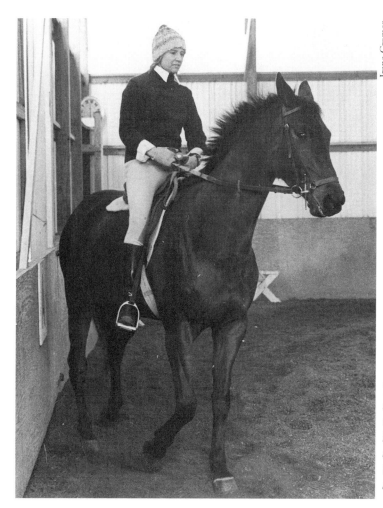

Irene Cromer

Too great an angle for shoulder-in. The horse is not bending in its body and is out of balance, stepping out of the track and into the arena.

and then develop the muscles. What you must strive for is a little progress in each exercise every day. Don't start them all at once; one leads to the next.

Shoulder-in is the foundation work. Done correctly, it strengthens the hind legs and increases their mobility and weight-carrying capacity. It also loosens up the shoulders, which improves the jumping. Increased suppleness brings lightness and obedience to the horse. It can be said that *shoulder-in is the cure for all ills, BUT (and it is a big but), only if done correctly.* Shoulder-in requires the horse to bring its shoulder to the inside of the track by *bending its body* and moving the inside hind leg under its mass. Merely bringing the shoulders in toward the center doesn't accomplish the same thing. Riders often bring the shoulders in, but let the hindquarters escape to the outside, thus avoiding any beneficial bending at all.

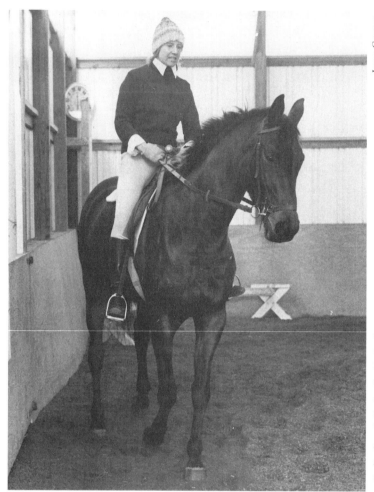

Irene Cromer

Better. The horse is on three tracks and reaching into the outside rein with the hindquarters on the track. A more "together" look, although the rider still has her weight a little too much to the inside.

The most common fault in riding a shoulder-in is seen when the rider tries to pull the forehand to the inside with the inside rein; this produces a bent head and neck, but nothing else. Any time the rider tries to do this movement with the rein alone, the horse loses rhythm, balance, and impulsion—all serious faults. The best way to think of shoulder-in is that the horse will increase its bend around the rider's inside leg and move onto the outside rein, which controls the amount of bending allowed. Whatever you create in the way of bending and energy with your inside leg, the outside hand will receive and control.

The easiest way to begin is to bring the horse out of a corner or off a circle and maintain the bend as you go down the track. The horse's hind legs remain on the track while its shoulders and forehand are to the inside. Your own shoulders remain parallel to the horse's shoulders; your outside shoulder will be in advance of the inside one and your weight moves slightly from the inside to the outside in the direction in which you are going.

Shoulder-in is the only lateral movement in which the horse is bent away from the direction it is traveling, that is, *bent left but traveling to the right,* and vice versa. Your inside hand should be in light contact and the horse must remain firmly in your outside hand. Your inside leg should be used gently in time with the horse's inside hind, encouraging it to step under the weight of the body. Your outside leg goes slightly behind the girth to keep the hindquarters from sliding to the outside and avoiding the bend, and also to prevent the outside leg from blocking the movement. If you use too much inside rein, you will also block the hind leg of the horse.

All "sideways" movements are described as "two-track" movements. In actuality, you will find that the shoulder-in is ridden as a "three-track" movement, with the first track being described by the outside hind leg, the second by the outside fore and inside hind, and the third by the inside fore. It should never be ridden at too great an angle so that all four legs are on separate tracks. It is really helpful to have a mirror to look into as you try this exercise. If you are having trouble, the chances are that it is because you are not sitting correctly and have your weight blocking the horse's movements. Sometimes riders try so hard they forget that the key to success is the correct position of the body and application of the aids. If you get your horse and yourself into the correct "shape," all movements will become much easier.

It is perhaps easiest to begin working on any new exercise at the walk, but as soon as you have the feel of it, go into the trot, as there is much less danger of losing the impulsion. Once you can do shoulder-in at trot, you can effectively use it at the canter also. I well remember the first time my instructor asked me to do this. I had to stop and think about it for a while; it seemed likely that my horse would cross its legs and fall flat on its face. But I was overjoyed to find that the exercise improved the balance in canter one hundredfold.

Half-pass demands even greater agility from the horse. The movement requires the bend to be in the direction the horse is traveling, with the hind leg flexing and stretching even more. The difficulty at first is in keeping the correct bend. Begin by riding a half-circle to the center line. Then, keeping the bend you have on the half-circle, ask the horse to move back to the track on two tracks. The horse is looking towards the track; your inside leg is on the girth, keeping the horse bent around it; your outside leg is behind the girth, asking the horse to move laterally. In effect, you are telling the horse, *"go forward,* and *over; forward and over."* If you lose the bend, the best cure is to ask for a couple of steps of shoulder-in as you complete the half-circle. Then ask for half-pass, then shoulder-in again so that you progress toward the track by going forward in shoulder-in and sideways in half-pass, alternately.

Haunches-in uses the same positioning as half-pass and is ridden down the side of the arena. The forehand stays on the track with the horse looking forward—never to the outside—and the hindquarters come slightly inside as the horse bends around the inside leg. When you practice any of the lateral movements, you should intersperse some vigorous forward movements, asking for a distinct lengthening of the stride. As the horse becomes more supple and shifts more of its weight from the forehand to the hindquarters, you will find it easier to shorten and lengthen the stride at will. Your horse is becoming educated.

Another excellent suppling and strengthening exercise is the counter-canter. In this exercise you ask the horse to canter, leading with the outside leg. Begin only when the horse is regular and steady in true canter.

At first, ride down the track in true canter, make a half-circle, and ride back to the track, retaining the same lead. Try to maintain the lead through the short end of the arena. The most common reaction is for the horse to rush or break. If you can keep your canter regular and forward, the horse will be able to do this more difficult exercise. It is a matter of balance. As long as the horse is in balance it can perform counter-canter, which really isn't that difficult. You must keep your aids consistent with the lead, not the direction. If, for instance, you are riding the horse in left lead canter, your left hip bone will be slightly forward, your left leg will be at the girth, and your right leg will be behind the girth, positioning the horse for left canter. As you ride your half-circle, *keep the same aids and look slightly to the left.* The horse remains bent to the left to keep the left lead. As you go through the corner, keep your weight to the left, and keep your right leg firmly behind the girth so that the horse understands that it must keep the left lead. Don't relax the aids. If you keep your head to the left, it will help you keep your weight in the correct place. Don't let your horse speed up to avoid the difficulty, as this causes it to lose its balance and break. Holding your hands a little higher than normal will help the horse keep its balance.

Your horse can learn to counter-canter in one lesson. It won't be very good counter-canter at first and will feel quite awkward, but if you practice daily you will find that the horse is able to canter figure-eights on one lead in either direction. Persevere until it becomes as easy to counter-canter as to canter true. Your horse's regular canter will reap great benefits. Remember, all this flat work is laying the foundation for your success in jumping.

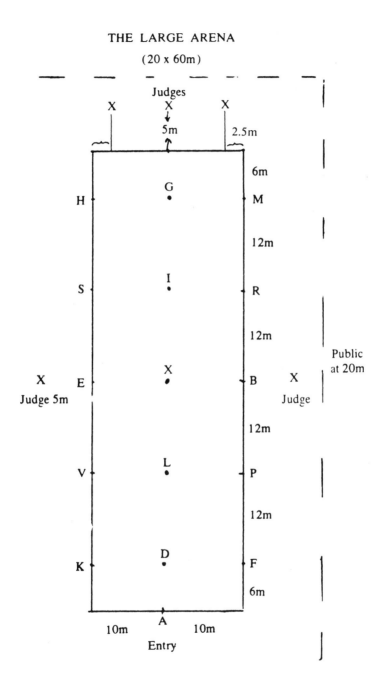

THE LARGE ARENA

(20 x 60m)

11
ADVANCED CAVALETTI WORK: GYMNASTICS

The conditioning you did at the Novice Level should now be extended over a greater amount of time as the horse will be facing longer, more challenging courses. Distances and speeds are stepped up and, as the fences get bigger, you take them at a greater rate of speed. This makes sense, as it is easier to jump a larger fence with more momentum. Horses that are not galloping have a hard time reaching out over a big fence. Your conditioning schedule is still based on interval training theories already discussed. You are not yet getting ready for a full three-day event, but all conditioning leads towards that goal.

When your horse has been in work for a month or so and can work for an hour and a half without becoming stressed unduly, you can begin to increase the demands in your jumping work. Cavaletti should be used at least once a week, and you can use both trotting and cantering formations to build muscle and balance. The trotting work encourages the horse to lower its head and neck and use its topline, which strengthens the back. The cantering gymnastics prepare the necessary muscles for later jumping work. Cantering combinations can be endlessly varied. Start with the fences 18' apart, allowing a short stride between jumping efforts. By keeping the distance at 18' feet, you put the horse into a short stride that encourages use of the back in a proper bascule. Your horse has already learned to do these cantering formations in earlier lessons, and you can now increase the demands by putting two cavaletti together to make small oxers, encouraging the horse to use its back even more. Set up a series of four or five of these and take them in both directions several times.

Again, don't overdo; don't bore the horse or overstress it. Bounces or no-strides really work the muscles in the hind legs. Set up a series of six cavaletti at 9' apart, and watch someone ride through them. See what a work-out the hocks get in this gymnastic?

As long as you use common sense, your horse's strength and ability will increase daily. Now set rails in front of small fences. Start with one set at 18' away, to put the horse into a correct take-off, and then progress to using a bounce rail at 9' before the fence to make the horse round over the fence. As your horse becomes more proficient, you can decrease the distance in front of the fence to 7 1/2 or 8 feet, but don't do this all at once, and don't use such a severe bounce more than three or four times in a lesson. The height of your fences should not exceed 3' for these exercises.

For horses that are inclined to rush, you can set up a series of fences which forces them to slow down and watch where they are going. It is likely that you are familiar with the term "poling." Many jumper trainers use this technique, which can be a dangerous and cruel practice. But by setting up a series of fences at short distances, you can effectively let the horse "pole" itself by hitting the solid rails. It will quickly learn not to hit a fence. Set a series of fences (at least four) consisting of a small cross-rail, then an oxer at 18', then another oxer at 21' (you need more distance on the second one as the horse will naturally lengthen its stride a little as it gathers momentum), and another oxer at 22'. These gymnastics do not need to be more than 3' high. For a really bad rusher, set a cavaletti at the lowest height on the ground halfway between each fence, that is, approximately 9' from the first and 10' from the second, etc. This has the effect of making the horse look down at the cavaletti to avoid landing on it, and teaches it to keep a round, short stride into a fence. It is a most effective way of slowing down a rushing horse.

You should be practicing making tight turns by placing one small jump at a right angle to another. Learn to control the horse's outside shoulder and to keep the hocks underneath the body. How often have you pulled the left rein to turn the horse to the left, only to have it go on boring out to the right?

You must control both shoulders of the horse and make the hindquarters follow the shoulders. Ride *both sides* of the horse and control *both ends*. It isn't as easy as it sounds, but then, whoever said that riding was easy?

Placing the cavaletti on the line of a circle can be useful for learning to ride through corners and over fences. Place four small jumps on a large circle and work around it until your horse keeps both the bend and the rhythm and you can negotiate a proper circle.

After two or three weeks of work on gymnastics, you can practice riding over a small course. Here again, pay attention to the problems that develop and consider ways to correct them. As I have said before, if you are having any trouble at this level, you are not ready to move up. Work on those problems now—don't think that they are going to disappear. They won't.

By the time you have spent five or six weeks on this preparatory work, you can start your conditioning program in earnest. It is time to take up the interval training again.

Each horse is slightly different and must have a slightly different schedule. Your cold-blooded, squarely-built horse will need more galloping than the rangy Thoroughbred which will need more muscle building. Consult Table 3 to help in drawing up your schedule.

Plan your calendar for each horse and fill in a schedule of work leading up to competitions. This gives you a guide and also a place to record your progress. Block out the competitions you have in mind for the season and plan to bring your horse to a "peak" at the time of the most important one. Most areas hold Training Level Championships annually, and your goal should be to try to qualify for and then compete in these. Include schooling shows, clinics, and minor events such as Pony Club affairs in your conditioning scheme, but remember your eventual goal and work towards it. Don't just haphazardly enter any and all events in your area. A horse cannot be brought along properly without a definite plan.

If all goes well, your horse should be ready for a one-day Training Level horse trial and be able to complete it without any trouble at all. Along with the conditioning work, you must continue your work in dressage and jumping. Your horse is becoming more educated as well as fitter than ever before, so you had better be out jogging, playing tennis, or doing some getting-fit exercises yourself; a fit horse is a handful, and you need to be in at least as good condition as your horse in order to stay in control.

12

CROSS COUNTRY OBSTACLES AND HOW TO RIDE THEM

Cross country jumping now becomes more challenging. Combinations, bigger and wider spreads, splash jumps, ditch and bank combinations all have to be tackled and the groundwork for future levels confirmed, first at the Training level and then at the Preliminary level. Different types of fences should be considered separately and schooled one at a time.

SPLASH FENCES

Splash fences seem to cause the most trouble to the horses in combined training, at all levels. Usually it is because the all-important first steps were either rushed through, or neglected entirely. Take the time to introduce your horse to water fences, ride them correctly, and you should have no trouble as you progress to higher levels.

At the Novice level, you should have been cantering through streams, and perhaps popping over small logs into water. At the Training level, however, you can expect to face drops into water as well as more complicated fences into or out of water. The horse's first introduction to streams should set the pattern for future work. It is good to have another horse along that can give you and your green horse a lead. Trot through the stream as many times as it takes to accustom your horse to thinking nothing of it. If you plan ahead carefully and do some scouting around, you can pick a place in a stream that offers a fairly wide crossing.

Carry in a cavaletti to make your first splash jump. Trot through until your horse is quite happy about the whole idea and then canter through at a good

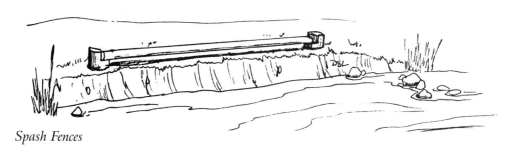

Spash Fences

Julie Jones

Have the horse canter through the water, jump out, and then jump a small fence afterwards.

ongoing pace. As soon as the horse has the idea, place your cavaletti or small jump at the far side of the crossing and jump *out of the water.* Make a great big fuss of your horse and let it know just how very clever it is. Horses take to strange jumps quite well but need plenty of encouragement from you.

The next step is to reverse the process. Approach from the far side of the cavaletti and jump *into the water,* again praising the horse abundantly. Do this several times, alternately jumping in and then out. If possible, place a cavaletti on both approach and exit. Then put your jump *in the middle of the water,* so that you enter the water, jump while still in the water, then exit.

Now, the same day, if at all possible, you should try your first *drop into water.* Find a place where you have to jump down about 2'6" to 3' into a stream, stretch of water or pond *with a firm bottom.* Again, have your experienced horse give a lead. Approach firmly, but fairly slowly. Any time you gallop flat out into water you risk a nasty spill. The water acts as a brake, your horse comes to a screeching stop, and off you go over its head. That's a refreshing bath on a hot day, but not a good idea in competition! You should

Reverse the process—jump the small jump and drop into the water.

The rider is too far forward which could cause a problem of balance.

Julie Jones

Walk fences at least three times and decide how to attack them.

Julie Jones

The horse is drifting to the left a little...   *but is concentrating on the far side of the water.*

repeat this exercise several times in order to impress the horse with the ease of it, then stop for that session.

The next time you school over water, you can use your cavaletti a couple of times, repeat your drop fence, then try to find a small obstacle perched on top of a drop. A log or something solid is best.

Most horses will take this more difficult task in their stride as long as you have not rushed them into it, but have done a slow, careful preparation. *The more air there is in a splash jump, the more difficult it is.* Big solid rails or logs into water are much more inviting to the horse. A rail fence with a view of the water through the rails is much more difficult. The horse should not be asked to do anything like this until the Preliminary Level. Fences with air going into water can cause a green horse to have severe qualms about the idea and can put them off forever. Once a horse starts stopping at water you have a real problem on your hands. *Don't ask the horse to do something it isn't ready for.* Be content to progress at a slow, steady rate.

Don't expect a green horse to jump perfectly—anything can and may happen!   *The second time is still unbalanced. You need to keep trying until the horse figures out the problem.*

Follow the leaders over a fence into the water.

A confident drop into a water complex.

All photos: Julie Jones

First drop into water. The horse hesitates to check the problem out...

...and decides to jump.

but has trouble with the landing gear. The rider is in a defensive seat to avoid a fall.

The second time, he is much braver...

and lands in balance, ready to go on.

A difficult drop into water. The horse is on a very steep angle. Rider has leaned back and actually dropped the reins entirely.

It is the stride after landing that is the most difficult.

Recovery and a focused drive to the next element.

All photos: Julie Jones

DITCHES

Here we encounter the second most common problem in cross-country, and again it is careful schooling that prevents refusals. We have already discussed introducing the horse to small ditches, now you can expect to have combination fences with ditches included. The difficulty of a ditch jump is in direct relation to its depth. The horse is more concerned with the depth than the width.

Ditches should be approached firmly by lengthening the stride once the horse has seen the obstacle. Do not gallop in so fast the horse does not have a chance to see the ditch until the last moment, when it may well slam on the brakes. If you increase pace into a ditch, it is obvious that you intend to fly over it. If you are hesitant, the horse might interpret it as a command to jump into the ditch instead of over it.

Try to ride up to the edge of a ditch as much as possible. If a horse stands back at a wide ditch, the width becomes tremendous and you risk the possibility of the hind legs falling into the ditch on the landing side, which can cause a dangerous situation.

A ditch with a fence in front of it is the easiest type. The horse will take the ditch in stride with its normal arc over the height of the fence. A ditch with a fence behind it is harder because the horse is not aware of the pres-

Julie Jones

Over a big ditch with ease.

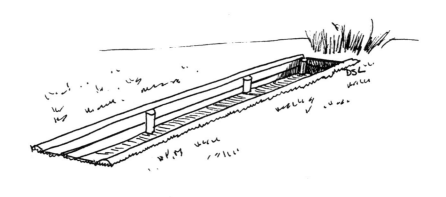

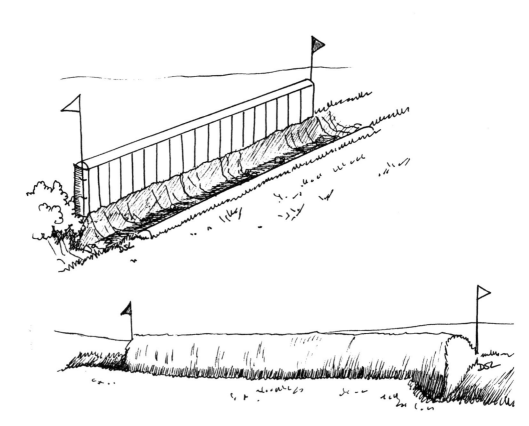

Ditches

ence of the ditch until the take-off stride. This type of obstacle must be ridden with great firmness—maybe even with a reminder from the stick that you mean business. When approaching a ditch before a jump up onto a bank, ride carefully to the edge, so that the horse can jump cleanly up onto the bank. A ditch on the far side of a bank rarely causes much trouble.

Bank Jumps

A combination of more advanced bank and drop from one level to another over a ditch.

BANK JUMPS

This type of obstacle is being included on more Training level courses and needs to be practiced at home before it is encountered in competition. A straightforward bank entailing a jump up onto the top, a stride or two, and then a drop off the other side should present little trouble. Jumping up is usually quite simple, but sometimes the horse will slam on the brakes at the far side. You must keep your leg on and, with your whole body, urge your

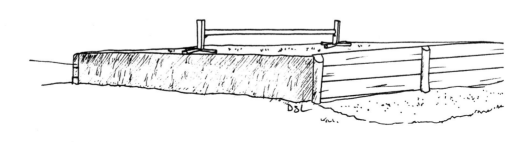

horse forward once you have made the jump up onto the bank. It has to learn to get its legs underneath its body quickly in order to be prepared for the take-off almost immediately after the initial effort. It is well to spend some time schooling over the easy banks, as the more complicated ones require some quick thinking on the part of the horse. Banks come in all shapes and sizes, with all sorts of different combinations of fences included.

Irish Bank

IRISH BANKS

These are usually natural banks, without the revetting of more formal banks. There is usually a ditch before or beyond the bank with perhaps another fence just after it. The horse must be ridden just as firmly at this, with tremendous determination on the part of the rider, so that it doesn't stop when it sees the fence coming up on the far side. It is necessary to keep the horse together on top so that it can stay off its forehand and get up and out over the fence at the far side.

Normandy Bank

NORMANDY BANKS

This usually includes a ditch in front of a bank, with a fence on the far side making a big drop in the second part. You have to be sure you make a correct approach to this type of obstacle. How fast you come at it depends on how much room you have on top before the second effort. A short distance on top means that your horse has to come in, jump up, get his legs under him and jump over the next part on the way off. It is imperative that you keep your legs on. You may even have to go to the bat if the horse hesitates on the first part. You can't afford to be left behind. If there is enough room for a stride or two on top you can afford to come a little stronger at the first element. If the horse hesitates, you must be quick to give him a sharp reminder that you won't tolerate any slowing down. Try to ride for the edge of the ditch so that your horse can reach up to the top of the bank comfortably and not catch his stifle on the edge. A horse with a very long stride needs to be steadied into this type of fence so that he has enough room to get his feet organized on top without coming up against the fence on the top.

DROP FENCES

The golden rule for drops—*never look down!* Time after time you see riders coming into drops and tensing up as they look down into a seemingly bottomless pit. Horses instinctively feel this reluctance on the part of the rider and slam on the brakes. Often the rider sails on over the fence—all alone! The best way to tackle a drop is to stay in the middle of the saddle,

Drop Fence

Drop Fence

urge your horse forward, and keep the forward drive throughout the approach. Some riders tend to lean backwards over a drop in case the horse pecks on landing. This is permissible, but you should never lean back until after the horse has left the ground and cleared the first part of the obstacle. Leaning back prematurely can cause the horse to drop its hind legs into the rails or whatever, and it's goodbye, horse and rider! Again, if you start off with small simple drops before facing your horse with stiffer ones, it should be quite willing to tackle anything you ask. Drop fences take their toll on the legs, so limit the number of drops you school over to a bare minimum. There's no point in schooling unnecessarily and risking injury. As long as the horse understands that drop fences are fairly simple, there is no need to practice endlessly.

Fences that have a drop as part of a combination are ridden exactly the same as a drop by itself. If there is a drop into water and then a fence in the water or on the other side, the drop should be ridden firmly out of a short, bouncy stride so that the landing impact is minimized. A drop onto flat terrain is always more jarring for a horse, while a drop onto ground that slopes away on the other side is easier. What you have to watch for on the latter type is that the ground is not wet or slippery on the landing side.

Being too far forward over a drop is worse than being too far back. The rider who is too forward runs the risk of pitching over the horse's head if there is any problem on landing. A *strong leg position with the heel pushed well down and a little forward* can keep you in the saddle if there is a slip or stumble on landing. If you have a vertical fence going downhill, you want to be sure your horse will take off early enough. If you get in too close, your horse will catch its knees and roll over. Standing back a little at this type of fence also reduces the height to be cleared. The reverse is also true; when you jump uphill, the closer you are to the fence, the less height the horse has to clear.

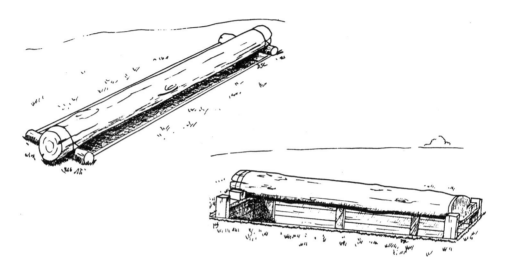

Trakehners

TRAKEHNERS AND FENCES WITH OPTICAL PROBLEMS FOR THE HORSE

A Trakehner is a fence with a big log or rail over a ditch. Here again, you want to concentrate on the log and encourage the horse to see the top of the fence. You don't want it to peer down into the ditch and stop. Once you have a refusal on this type of jump, you are in trouble, as the appearance of the ditch can really scare a horse once it realizes what is there. A Trakehner needs to be ridden at a good rate of speed. Encourage the horse to make a bold approach, *increasing* rather than *decreasing* the speed as you get close to the fence. Ask for a big, bold leap. Think of it as jumping a large, free-standing rail, and forget the ditch is there. Come in to a previously chosen take-off point, and ride for a big fence. If your horse hesitates, give it a sharp tap with the bat as a reminder to get on with the job. Don't wait to see what the horse is going to do—if there is a fraction of doubt in your mind, whap it a good one. *Determination* on the part of the rider is transmitted to the horse immediately, *so is hesitation!*

Julie Jones

A log over a ditch or simple trakhener.

COMBINATIONS

Combination obstacles are often planned to present the rider with optional approaches. You have to consider your horse carefully when making your plan for riding as you walk the course. Does your horse have a big jump? In that case, if there is an optional big oxer or spread, go for that. It's only one jumping effort and is going to save time and energy. However, if your horse is still green and you think the big fence is a bit too much at its present stage

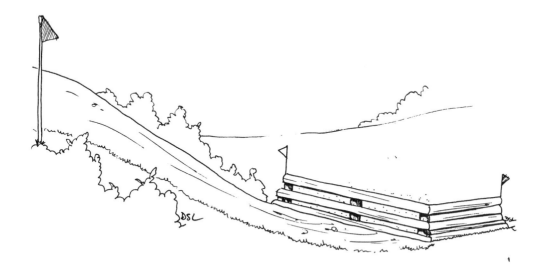

Combination

of training, go for the more conservative route, perhaps through the middle, with a single stride. Pace off all distances *very carefully,* and pick the distance that suits your particular horse's stride.

Depending on the course, combinations using one stride can vary from 18 to 26 feet. Remember that an in-and-out set on a downward slope tends to be shorter than you think. The greater momentum you gather jumping downhill tends to make the horse land further out than it would if it was on the flat. A typical example of this was the fence at Ship's Quarters in Maryland that was set on the hill and offered a corner, then a vertical fence down the slope. Many horses came to grief by jumping too big over the first element and chesting out on the second. The longer way takes a little more time, but it is a great deal safer!

BOUNCES

A bounce is a fence that entails two jumping efforts without a stride in between; the horse jumps the first fence and immediately takes off again for the second. Your work with cavaletti prepares the horse for this type of fence. Set your cavaletti, on the highest setting, at 9' intervals and let the horse "bounce" through in a nice rhythm. As you progress, you can alter the height of your bounce strides by using two rails, set up at 2 '9", and placed 9 or 10 feet apart. This can still be taken from a trot, letting the horse find out just where it is supposed to put its feet. As soon as it knows how to cope

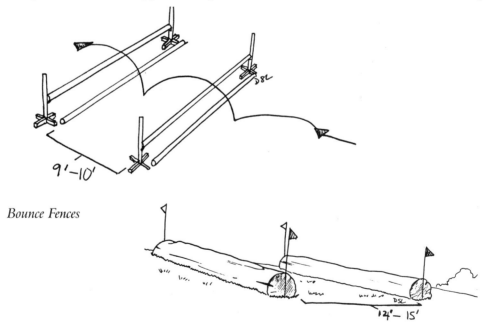

Bounce Fences

with this, you can set fences at 3' high and 12' apart and canter in at 400 to 450 meters per minute. Lots of patting and praising the horse when it accomplishes this new task is an important part of your training program. A horse must build confidence in its rider if it is expected to jump unhesitatingly, even when it can't see the landing. Your horse must develop complete trust in you. A rider who is not certain of his or her desire to get to the other side of a fence will never be able to convince a horse to do so.

Riding a bounce demands that you approach at a very short canter, in order to keep the horse round. Never flatten out, as jumping big can land the horse chest-high to the second element. Show jumping technique, demanding a very controlled approach, is the order of the day. Be sure to be up with the horse, and maintain the contact and forward drive to help it on the other side.

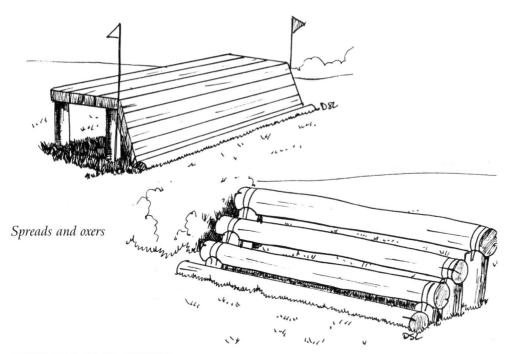

Spreads and oxers

SPREADS AND OXERS

A spread fence requires an accurate approach, with a take off as close to the first rail as possible, without getting under it. Don't let your horse take off miles away — this only increases the width of the fence and begs for a fall.

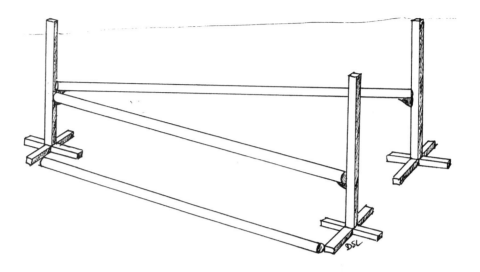

ANGLES AND CORNERS

Often the shortest distance between two points requires you to take a jump at an angle in order to make the distances right, or to jump the corner of an obstacle to make one effort instead of two. You can school for this in your stadium arena.

When your horse is jumping confidently on a straight approach at the required heights, you can school it to take fences at an angle. Using an upright jump, approach at a slight angle and pop over it. The trick is to convince the horse to *keep the line of approach constant.* You can practice this when you are schooling the stadium fences and, if you are careful and consistent, you will find that the horse takes to approaching fences at angles up to 45 degrees quite happily, as long as you are careful with your approach. When you can take the angled approach, then set a second jump at an angle to the first. The standards will help tremendously by giving the horse a natural wing. Keep the fences low, 2'6" to 2'9" at first, and the angle between the two *relatively small.* Once the horse accepts this new idea, you can gradually increase the height and the angle. But be sure that the horse is accustomed to coming in at an angle before you increase the difficulty of the exercise.

All of the obstacles you meet with on the cross-country course are variations of these basic types. Although they may look formidable, when analyzed they reduce to basic jumping efforts. The knowledgeable rider will prepare his or her horse to face all types of problems and solve them readily.

13
MORE STADIUM WORK

At the Novice level, the stadium courses were simple and straightforward. As you move up to the Training level, you can expect to have more difficult courses, with more turns, and you must be prepared to take combination fences. With your practice over gymnastic formations, however, this should present no problems. At this point, the idea is to show the horse that combinations are nothing to get excited about. From your use of take-off rails and bounces, as discussed earlier, it should be quite capable of making multiple jumping efforts, one after the other.

Simple combinations are in-and-outs, usually set at 24' to 26'. In your schooling you have been using shorter distances, 18', in order to make the horse use its back and develop its muscles, but in jumping a complete course where you will be expected to move on a bit more at the fences, the longer distances are more correct.

The easiest combination consists of an upright fence followed by a spread or oxer. Two uprights are more difficult, an oxer followed by an upright even more so, and two oxers are the most difficult of all. The chart provided gives an idea of the degree of difficulty in combinations, and you can prepare the horse gradually by using each of them in your schooling sessions. It goes without saying that all fences used for schooling stadium should be solid and imposing so that the horse will not take chances with them.

All too often, the whole event has been lost in the stadium phase. I remember sitting at Badminton, watching Mary Thompson of Great Britain enter the arena in sole possession of first place in the Three-Day competition. There was a group of Brits sitting in front of us with whom we had struck up a conversation. "There you are, there's your winner," I remarked

Combinations in ascending degree of difficulty.

Doubles

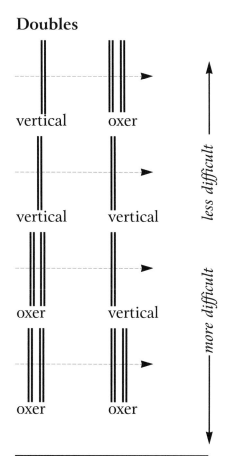

Triples

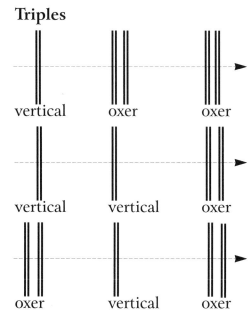

Ramped oxers where the back rail is one hole higher are easier than completely square ones with the rails at the same height.

Too dificult for lower levels:

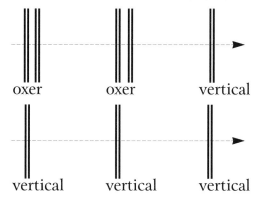

as King William came in on a loose rein, looking for all the world as if he were about to start another outstanding dressage test. "Oh no," came the reply. "He's no good at this." Sure enough, King William pulled rails off three fences, dropping Mary to third place.

It isn't enough to just work at your gymnastics and single fences. You must practice riding whole courses. Go to local hunter-jumper shows and enter the Junior Jumper or Warm-up Jumper classes to gain experience. Your horse should be able to cope with a solid 3'6" course in order to complete Training Level courses at 3'3".

Riding the line of the course so that your horse is properly presented to each fence takes some practice. The rider's job in jumping is to put the horse in the correct speed and frame, and to bring it to the fence in good balance. Leave the jumping up to the horse—it jumps the fence—all you do is regulate what happens in between. Ninety percent of the mistakes you see in the ring are caused by riders. You must put in time practicing in order to perform well. Watch some of the top competitors and you will see perfect examples of the rider controlling every step and bringing the horse to the best possible spot to negotiate the fence.

If you have trouble seeing distances, train yourself with outside aids. Set markers (flags, standards, something like that) at one, two, or three strides from the fence and teach yourself to bring the horse in correctly. Practice your turns by putting a pole to turn around at a distance of three strides from the fence.

By using take-off rails as you did in the early training of the horse, you can develop its sense of distance. A horse that is properly trained will cope with the jumps well as long as you do your part in dictating the correct speed and length of stride. By the time you get to Training Level, you should be confident in your ability. The horse should trust you and enjoy jumping. Too often, riders jump and jump until the horse gets sore, sour, and fed up with the whole idea. If you plan your jumping sessions each week and do constructive work at each one, rewarding the horse as soon as it does what is required, there is no need to spend hours and hours schooling over fences.

Your jumping sessions should include some strange looking fences, as well as straight poles. There is absolutely no excuse for a horse who refuses brick walls and brightly painted panels simply because you haven't bothered to practice over similar obstacles. Put your ingenuity to work and use all sorts of objects in your stadium courses. As a result, your horse won't be at all surprised by the pots of flowers in the stadium at your next event.

It is essential that you find something to represent water. The best horses in the world will gawk at water in a stadium ring. At home, use a plastic

Rider is ahead of the movement. Needs some weight in heel and a more flexible arm.

Behind the motion but allowing the horse to stretch neck.

Too long a stirrup creates a weak position lacking stability.

Riders has been badly left behind and is using rein for balance—horse is therefore totally

Horse jumping long and flat—rider needs to have firm lower leg to make the horse jump rounder.

Better balance between horse and rider.

sheet or garbage bag, fastened down, to simulate water, or dig a shallow ditch and fill it up with the real thing. I've seen more refusals and eliminations in Training Level stadium jumping because of water than because of any other single type of fence.

Your horse should be able to jump a simple water jump with no height, and any type of fence with water in front, in the middle, or behind it, without thinking twice. All it takes is a proper introduction. If you can spend your time on schooling for splash jumps cross country, you can take the same time to school for water in stadium. It can mean the difference between a ribbon and an elimination!

Before riding your stadium round at a competition, take the time to warm up properly. Don't just take one fence and then sit and wait. Let your horse know that it is doing a job, and that you mean business.

Many horses get very excited about the stadium, as they think they are still going cross country. The only way to convince them otherwise is to expose them to show jumping conditions in as many different places as you can so that they become calm about it. This is where your local hunter-jumper shows come in handy. If you use them as a training ground, your horse should be quite used to jumping strange fences without undue fuss.

The same rules apply here as in the dressage phase: your horse must be calm, straight, and forward-going if you are to do a good job. All of that time spent on flat work should pay off when your horse goes around the stadium course, turning easily from hand and leg, and shortening and lengthening stride as necessary.

Pass Schedule.

TABLE 3
Conditioning Program for Training Level

7 WEEK SCHEDULE

WEEK 1

Day 1   One hour energetic walk on hills. Three 5-minute trots with 3 minute walk intervals.
Check PR, walk 10 minutes, check PR again. Write down the numbers when you get home.
NOTE: *Throughout all interval training, use a 3-minute walk between repetitions.*

Day 2   One hour dressage. One hour walk.

Day 3   30 minutes dressage. 30 minutes cavaletti work.

Day 4   45 minutes dressage. 45 minutes walk on hills.

Day 5   30 minutes dressage. One hour hack.
Include three 5-minute trots.
Include one 4-minute canter at 400 mpm (1600 meters). Check PR, walk 10 minutes, check recovery.

Day 6   30 minutes dressage. 30 minutes cavaletti gymnastics.

Day 7   Rest. Turn out.

WEEK 2

Day 1   30 minutes dressage. One and a half hour hack, including trotting on hills up to 15 minutes.

Day 2   30 minutes dressage. One hour hack.
Three 5-minute trots.
One 4-minute canter at 400 mpm (1600 meters).
Check PR. NOTE: *If at this point the PR is not dropping significantly in 10 minutes, by at least one half, you need to stay at this level until it does. Don't increase the work until the horse is doing this easily and recovering well.*

Day 3   30 minutes dressage. One hour walk.

Day 4   30 minutes dressage. 30 minutes cavaletti work.

Day 5   30 minutes dressage. One and a half hour walk on hills.

Day 6   30 minute hack.
Three 5-minute trots.
One 6-minute canter at 400 mpm (240 meters).
Check PR.

Day 7   Rest.

WEEK 3

Day 1   One hour dressage. One hour hack.

Day 2   30 minutes dressage. Practice some individual stadium fences up to 3'.

Day 3   30 minutes dressage. 30 minute hack.
Three 5-minute trots.
Two 4-minute canters at 400 mpm (1600 meters).
Check PR

Day 4   30 minutes dressage. One hour walk.

Day 5   30 minutes dressage. Cavaletti and stadium jumps.

Day 6   30 minutes hack. Three 5-minute trots.
Two 4-minute canters at 400 mpm.
One 6-minute canter at 400 mpm.
Check PR. (See Note, Week 2, Day 2).

Day 7   Rest.

WEEK 4

Day 1   One and a half hour walk on hills.

Day 2   One hour dressage, practice test for competition.

Day 3   30 minute hack. Three 5-minute trots.
Three 4-minute canters at 400 mpm. Check PR.

Day 4   School stadium jumping course up to 3'3".

Day 5   One and a half hour walk.
Day 6   30 minute walk. Three 5-minute trots.
        Three 4-minute canters at 400 mpm, OR, Hunter schooling show, maximum of three courses.
        Check PR.
Day 7   Rest.

WEEK 5
Day 1   Two hour walk.
Day 2   One hour dressage, work on your worst problems.
Day 3   30 minute walk. Three 5-minute trots.
        Two 4-minute canters at 400.
        One 6-minute canter. Check PR.
        NOTE: *If your PR recovery is good at this point, your horse is easily capable of doing a Training level horse trial.*
Day 4   30 minutes dressage. One and a half hour hack, including trotting on hills.
Day 5   30 minutes dressage. Cavaletti gymnastics.
Day 6   Two hour hack, OR
        Hunter schooling show, maximum of 3 courses, OR Local dressage show, First level classes.
Day 7   Rest.

WEEK 6
Day 1   Two hour hack.
Day 2   30 minutes dressage. Stadium jumping practice up to 3'3".
Day 3   30 minute hack. Three 5-minute trots.
        Two 4-minute canters at 400 mpm.
        One 6-minute canter at 450 mpm.
Day 4   30 minutes dressage. One hour walk.
Day 5   30 minutes dressage. 30 minutes cavaletti.
Day 6   30 minute walk. Three 5-minute trots.
        Two 4-minute canters at 400 mpm.
        One 6-minute canter at 400 mpm.
Day 7   Rest.

WEEK 7
Day 1   30 minutes dressage. One hour hack.
Day 2   30 minutes dressage. Stadium fences up to 3'3".
Day 3   30 minute hack. Three 5-minute trots.
        Two 4-minute canters at 400 mpm.
        One 6-minute canter at 450 mpm.
Day 4   Two hour walk.
Day 5   Practice dressage test.
Day 6   First Horse Trials.
Day 7   Rest.

14

PRELIMINARY REQUIREMENTS

The Preliminary horse is no longer a beginner. It has been through at least one year of competition, maybe even 18 months, and has been exposed to the tasks involved. Both rider and horse have some mileage behind them. Now is the time to make the important assessment of your horse's capabilities.

Not all horses can make the shift from competing in horse trials to competing in three-day events. The two contests are almost totally different sports. You should plan on a year's competition at Preliminary level before thinking about a Preliminary Three-Day Event. You have to decide whether your horse can really cope with a full-scale three-day competition. So far you have been taking cross-country courses of up to two miles; a full-scale event will include an endurance phase of 10 to 11 miles. That's a big step.

Whatever problems you have had at the Training level will be multiplied by the time you get to Preliminary, so sit down, list your horse's good points and shortcomings, and be brutally frank in your appraisal. If you are having trouble jumping Training level fences, you certainly are not ready for Preliminary ones. If you have had a hard time meeting the required speeds at Training level, you must face the fact that Preliminary courses are ridden at 520 meters per minute—considerably faster than the 400 or 450 mpm you have been going. Fences are bigger, wider, and more complicated.

Dressage is not much more difficult, but a greater degree of sophistication is required. The crux of the matter is whether you think your horse has the ability to handle the distances and speeds. Not all horses can. Riders are not always objective about their horses. Perhaps they don't realize the difference between horse trials and three-day events.

DRESSAGE

The dressage test used at the Preliminary level requires smaller circles, thus greater suppleness and balance, and a greater degree of impulsion. You must be more accurate; imprecise transitions are no longer tolerated. The horse should be confirmed on the bit, moving with lots of impulsion and more brilliance than before. Lengthening and shortening of the frame in trot and canter are asked for during the ride, and a high degree of polish is necessary if you are to score well. Let's face it, competition is so tough nowadays that a good score in dressage is almost a prerequisite for a ribbon.

Your schooling should be progressing along with the lines laid down in the previous chapter, with a great deal of attention paid to the lateral work to develop the necessary suppleness that improves performance. Your horse must be light, calm, and straight and should move with precision and impulsion. Mere relaxation is no longer enough.

CROSS COUNTRY

The basic types of fences met will be of a greater variety and not every fence will have a straightforward approach. Many more obstacles will be "rider problems" which require correct approach and careful thought. The horse must be able to handle complicated combinations. Jumps become bigger and wider and test courage and obedience. Courses will be longer and must be negotiated at greater speeds. Your conditioning will be stepped up and will take longer to achieve. You have to consider riding the roads and tracks phases and you will also have to learn how to ride a steeplechase course.

Julie Jones

Balanced on hindquarters and covering ground. Short stirrups and a steady body position.

STADIUM JUMPING

Again, this means bigger fences, more problems, and a greater test of horse and rider. This is the phase that riders often neglect, perhaps because there is so much other work to be done. It is just as important to learn how to jump the bigger stadium courses as it is to learn to deal with the cross country requirements. Yet, you cannot jump your horse every day. Your basic work will not change much. You must still use the cavaletti and gymnastics to work and develop the horse's muscles, but your practice sessions should include some bigger fences once in a while so that there are no problems when you face them in competition.

15

STEEPLECHASE

The one new skill you need to acquire is that of riding the steeplechase phase. Preparing the horse for this is not very complicated, but it is a part of training that is often neglected by first-time three-day riders. Incredibly enough, riders turn up at Preliminary three-day events *without ever having ridden a steeplechase fence at steeplechase speed.* This often leads, due to lack of judgement, to bad riding, abuse of horses, and bad falls.

Riding a steeplechase course is really quite simple, and fun. The secret lies in learning how to do it well. The three important facts you must bear in mind are: one, you must teach your horse to lengthen its stride at the gallop; two, the horse must move on at a greater rate of speed without scurrying and using unnecessary energy; and three, the horse must learn to jump at this faster speed.

After your horse has been in conditioning work for six weeks, begin the steeplechase training. The ideal way to teach the horse to gallop at steeplechase speed is to find a training track or race course that you can use. Many training farms are receptive to the idea of letting people train over the track, provided the race horses are done for the day. If you do not have access to a track, you will have to find a nice, level field with a good, straight stretch of a half-mile, if possible. Wherever you have been doing your interval training will serve if you have nowhere else. The trick is to get your horse to relax and stay calm during this work.

Horses come in two basic temperaments: those who rush and those who are lazy. The first type you should train alone to keep control; the second will profit from having a pacemaker along to give some incentive.

Typical flat jump over steeplechase brush fence.

Begin with a short gallop at about 400 meters per minute and, after a quarter-mile, increase speed gradually until you are cruising along at about 520 mpm for the next quarter-mile. Then, increase up to your required speed of 640 mpm, which is considerably faster than you have been going, and maintain this speed for a half-mile. Next, reverse the process for the next quarter-mile until you can pull down into a trot, then walk. Check your watch and see how close you came to the ideal time.

The most important part of this lesson is teaching your horse to increase speed calmly and steadily and maintain an even, relaxed gallop. There will be more rein contact than you have been using, but the horse must not fight it. You should have shorter stirrups than on the cross country and must take a firm rein contact, remaining forward throughout the whole exercise. The shorter stirrup may well give you some aching muscles. The front of the thigh and down the front of the shin can become quite painful at first but, if you continue, these aches will decrease as you get fitter. You need to develop your muscles as well as the horse's, and practice in the galloping phases will stand you in good stead in the cross country by making your legs and back much stronger.

You don't need to practice your steeplechase very often; once a month is more than sufficient, and a full-speed workout once every two weeks is fine. The main thing is that you and the horse learn to adjust to the greater

Landing well out over the steeplechase fence.

speeds and move in rhythm. Just as in the flat work, rhythm and balance make everything work so much more easily.

Once you can cope with a gallop of a half-mile or so at the proper rate, 640 meters per minute, you must learn to jump at that speed.

First-time three-day riders often come a cropper over the fences. I can remember a friend asking me at a three-day event how to ride the steeplechase fences. Not realizing that he really had never done it before, I blithely remarked, *"Oh,* just go flat out—you'll make the time easy." Well, he took me at my word and went flat out—he also went head over heels at the very first fence. Needless to say, that is not the idea.

Horses that have learned to jump cross country need little schooling over steeplechase fences. All that matters is that they stay calm and learn to stand off and jump slightly flatter than they have been doing. The rider's job is to keep the speed and rhythm and not worry about an exact takeoff. Speed nearly always produces a long jump and the horse will learn to stand back at its fences.

To practice, you need a sloping brush jump, about 3'9" to 4' high or, if at all possible, two, set about 250 meters apart. If you can only scrape up one, that is better than nothing. There should be a straight approach of not less than 100-150 meters. Start by jumping the fence at a speed of 450 meters, and then try it at about 520, which is the Preliminary cross country

Brushing through the top of the steeplechase fence.

speed. This way the horse will have time to familiarize itself with the fence and will relax. Too often, the first time around a steeplechase course produces spastic-looking jumps with the horse stopping in its tracks and taking a lurching up-and-down jump. The ideal is to flow over the fence without breaking the stride and rhythm of the gallop, landing reaching out for the next stride. When the horse has taken the fence well at the slower speeds, increase *gradually* on the flat until you reach 640 meters per minute, then go again. After a few times, the horse will get the idea and settle into the job.

The actual riding of the steeplechase during a three-day event will be discussed in conjunction with the entire competition. Now your job is to teach your horse the necessary skills.

If you have a sluggish horse, it will really help to practice with a companion. You can then gallop head to head with a more experienced horse, which will give your mount some competition and incentive. When you start to gallop over the fences it is important that you stay side by side. Often a horse takes a take-off cue from its companion, and if you are half a length or a length behind, you may find yourself taking off at an impossible distance and crashing into the fence. After a few practices you should then do the exercise alone so that your horse eventually gets used to going by itself.

Horses that get excited and rush should be allowed to go at their own speed. Stay passive and calm on the approach and, upon landing, check the rate of speed. By fighting on the approach, you only excite your horse. Further, a rider who is calm and in balance will steady a horse more quickly than anything else.

16

CONDITIONING FOR A PRELIMINARY THREE-DAY EVENT

Presumably your horse has had a vacation after the season of Training Level competition. Plan on spending a month bringing it back into good enough condition to start serious work again. Follow a plan of lungeing, hacking out, and working up and down hills until you are riding for a good hour and a half a day. Only then are you ready to begin strenuous conditioning.

The three months leading up to your first three-day event should include interval training and competition—at least four—horse trials at the Preliminary Level.

Having taken care of the routine veterinary matters such as shots, worming, etc., you have spent that month gradually building the horse up. Now it has been trotting for 15 minute periods and working in dressage for the last week. The following is a schedule for a horse that has competed well at the Training Level (perhaps even placing at the Training Level Championships the previous season). One caution at this point: you are going to be doing more galloping work now in order to get ready for your first three-day event and your horse must stay sound. For this reason, you will probably not do as much jumping as you did in earlier training. By now your horse should be able to jump a course without difficulty, so keep the schooling to a minimum.

Table 4
Conditioning Program for Preliminary Three-Day Event

15 WEEK SCHEDULE

WEEK 1

Day 1   Walk out for an hour and a half. Include three 5-minute trots with 3-minute intervals of walk. NOTE: *Throughout all interval training, use a 3-minute walk between repetitions.*

Day 2   30 minute hack. Three 5-minute trots. One 4-minute canter at 400 mpm (1600 meters). Check PR and make a note of numbers after 10 minutes.

Day 3   30 minutes dressage. One hour walk.

Day 4   Dressage: lateral work, lengthening and shortening of strides. 15 minutes cavaletti work.

Day 5   30 minutes dressage. One hour hack.

Day 6   Local hunter or dressage show; three classes maximum.

Day 7   Rest.

WEEK 2

Day 1   One and a half hour hack. One 15-minute trot.

Day 2   Dressage. 15 minutes cavaletti work.

Day 3   30 minute hack. Three 5-minute trots. Two 4-minute canters at 400 mpm (1600 meters).

Day 4   Dressage. One hour walk.

Day 5   Dressage. One hour hack, including hills.

Day 6   Local hunter show.

Day 7   Rest.

WEEK 3

Day 1   Two hour hack, including hills. One 15 minute trot.

Day 2   Dressage. School gymnastics.

Day 3   30 minute hack. Three 5-minute trots. Two 4-minute canters at 400 mpm (1600 meters).

Day 3   One 4-minute canter at 520 mpm (2080 meters or 1.26 miles). Check PR carefully.

Day 4   One and a half hour walk.

Day 5   Dressage.

Day 6   School over cross country fences at Training level height.

Day 7   Rest.

WEEK 4

Day 1   Two hour hack. 15 minutes trot up and down hills.

Day 2   Dressage. Work on canter transtions and lengthenings.

Day 3   30 minute hack. Three 5-minute trots. One 4-minute canter at 400 mpm. One 6-minute canter at 400 mpm. One 4-minute canter at 400 mpm.

Day 4   Dressage. 30 minutes cavaletti.

Day 5   One hour walk.

Day 6   Local hunter-jumper show. Do larger courses—up to 3'6".

Day 7   Rest.

WEEK 5

Day 1   Two hour hack. 30 minutes trotting on hills.

Day 2   Dressage. One hour walk.

Day 3   30 minute hack. Three 5-minute trots. Two 4-minute canters at 400 mpm. Then practice steeplechase speed: canter 400 meters at 400 mpm. Increase over the next 400 meters to 640 mpm. Canter 800 meters at 640 mpm (1 minute 15 seconds). Decrease over next 400 meters, then walk. Check PR. Walk 10 minutes and recheck.

Day 4   One and a half hour walk.

Day 5   Dressage. School cavaletti.

Day 6   Dressage show, First and Second levels tests.

Day 7   Rest.

WEEK 6
Day 1   Two hour hack.
         30 minutes trotting on hills.
Day 2   Dressage. Gymnastics.
Day 3   30 minute hack.
         Three 5-minute trots.
         One 4-minute canter at 400 mpm.
         One 6-minute canter at 450 mpm.
         One 6-minute canter at 400 mpm.
Day 4   One and a half hour walk.
Day 5   Dressage or ship to first
         Preliminary horse trials.
Day 6   Preliminary horse trials.
Day 7   Jog in hand for soundness. Rest.

WEEK 7
Day 1   One and a half hour walk on hills.
Day 2   Dressage. One hour hack.
Day 3   Dressage. One hour walk.
Day 4   Dressage. One and a half hour
         hack. 30 minutes trotting.
Day 5   Dressage. 15 minutes cavaletti.
Day 6   30 minute hack.
         Three 5-minute trots.
         One 4-minute canter at 400 mpm.
         Second steeplechase practice: 400
         meters at 400 mpm. Increase to
         640 mpm, 1600 meters (1 mile).
         This should take 2 minutes 30 sec-
         onds. Slow up over next 80 meters.
Day 7   Rest.

WEEK 8
Day 1   Two hour hack,
         30 minutes trotting.
Day 2   Dressage. One hour walk.
Day 3   30 minute hack.
         Three 5-minute trots.
         One 4-minute canter at 400 mpm.
         One 6-minute canter at 520 mpm.
         One 6-minute canter at 450 mpm.
         NOTE: *If your PR is not dropping by
         at least half in the 10 minute break,
         you are doing too much. Go back to
         the level where the PR did drop and
         work up gradually to this level.*
Day 4   Dressage. School cross country
         jumps up to 3'6".
Day 5   One and a half hour walk.

Day 6   Local hunter show.
Day 7   Rest.

WEEK 9
Day 1   Two hour hack,
         30 minutes trotting.
Day 2   Dressage. One hour walk.
Day 3   30 minute hack.
         Three 5-minute trots.
         Two 4-minute canters at 400 mpm.
         One 6-minute canter at 520 mpm
         (3120 meters).
Day 4   One and a half hour walk.
Day 5   Dressage or ship to Preliminary
         horse trials.
Day 6   Preliminary horse trials.
Day 7   Rest.

WEEK 10
Day 1   One hour walk.
Day 2   Dressage. One hour hack.
Day 3   Dressage. School gymnastics 30
         minutes.
Day 4   One and a half hour hack
Day 5   Dressage. One hour walk.
Day 6   If you need to school steeplechase
         speeds, do so now. Otherwise, one
         and a half hour hack.
Day 7   Rest.

WEEK 11
Day 1   Two hour hack,
         30 minutes trotting.
Day 2   Dressage. One hour walk.
Day 3   30 minute hack.
         Three 5-minute trots.
         One 4-minute canter at 400 mpm.
         Two 6-minute canters at 520 mpm.
Day 4   Two hour walk.
Day 5   Dressage. One hour walk.
Day 6   School stadium or local hunter-
         jumper show, courses at 3'6".
Day 7   Rest.

WEEK 12
Day 1   Two hour hack,
         30 minutes trotting.
Day 2   Dressage. One hour walk.

Day 3   30-minute hack.
         Three 5-minute trots.
         Two 4-minute canters at 400 mpm.
         School 1600 meters at steeplechase
         speed over brush fences (if you
         have only one fence, school a very
         large circle, taking fence at least
         three times). Cover 1600 meters
         in 2 minutes 30 seconds. Pull up
         gradually over 800 meters.
         As always, check PR.
Day 4   Two hour walk.
Day 5   Dressage or ship to Preliminary
         horse trials.
Day 6   Preliminary horse trials.
Day 7   Rest.

WEEK 13
Day 1   One hour walk.
Day 2   Two hour hack,
         15 minutes trotting.
Day 3   Dressage. One hour walk.
Day 4   Dressage. Cavaletti.
Day 5   30 minute hack.
         Three 5-minutes trots.
         One 4-minute canter at 450 mpm.
         Two 6-minute canters at 520 mpm.
Day 6   School gymnastics and stadium.
Day 7   Rest.

WEEK 14
Day 1   Two hour hack. Trotting on hills.
Day 2   Dressage. Gymnastics.
Day 3   30 minute hack.
         Three 5-minute trots.
         One 5-minute canter at 400 mpm.
         One 8-minute canter at 520 mpm,
         increase to 640 mpm at 4 minutes;
         canter 2 minutes at this speed,
         then back down to 520 for
         remaining 2 minutes.
         One 4-minute canter at 400 mpm.
         NOTE: *Your PR should be dropping
         after 10 minutes even with the faster
         speeds.*
Day 4   Two hour walk.
Day 5   Dressage. One hour walk.
Day 6   School stadium courses up to 3'9''.
Day 7   Rest.

WEEK 15
Day 1   Dressage. One hour walk.
Day 2   Dressage. Cavaletti.
Day 3   Ship to three-day event.
         Work 45 minutes dressage.
         30 minutes walk.
Day 4   First three-day event.
Day 5   Three-day event.
Day 6   Three-day event.
Day 7   Jog for soundness. Rest.

Of course, it is all very well to sit at a typewriter and work out a schedule like this, but it never works in real life. You will find that no matter how hard you try to stay with your carefully planned program, things are always interfering. Your horse loses a shoe and you can't get the blacksmith for three days—forfeit three days of training. Your horse gets a minor injury—forfeit one week. Also, the vagaries of the Omnibus schedule make it impossible to get to four Preliminary horse trials, and so it goes. If we could only schedule life as we want it, everything would be so simple!

This outline is to give you an idea of just how much work has to be done if your horse is to be properly prepared for its first three-day event. There are ways to get around certain injuries, hard ground, etc. For instance, you can swim your horse instead of galloping. Make sure you have a safe place to do it, as some horses do not take kindly to such exercise and you could risk further injury. Still, many horses have swum their way to success. Swimming is tremendous effort: one minute of swimming is the equivalent of a mile gallop. Remember that walking builds muscles, and that hills can also be used to good effect.

It is, perhaps, as easy to overtrain as to undertrain. If your horse gets sour or too tight, back off some of the galloping work in your schedule. As a rule of thumb, your horse should be able to gallop comfortably three times the length of the cross country course at the three-day event you plan to attend. The length of the course will be published in Omnibus schedule so you can look it up and plan accordingly. Divide the length of the course by the speed of 520 mph. If the published length is 4,500 meters, that will take 8 minutes 38 seconds. If your horse is capable of doing three times that distance in his conditioning, you should have no problem with the roads and tracks and steeplechase added to that distance.

Watch the feeding carefully to be sure your horse is getting enough hard feed, but don't overdo it and end up with an unmanageable horse.

Some horses need more fast work than outlined here. If this is the case with yours, increase the length of each interval at 520 by one or two minutes, but do not go over 10 minutes for even the coldest blooded horse. If the steeplechase speed is difficult for your horse, try working with a companion as a pacemaker. If even that doesn't seem to help, you may have to face the fact that your horse just isn't fast enough. Perhaps you should just stay at the Preliminary horse trials stage.

On the other hand, some horses get fit quickly and may not need many fast workouts, but more slower ones to build stamina. Remember you will be going a total of 10 to 11 miles in your three-day event, so the more long, slow miles you put on your horse, the better prepared it will be. The speed work is primarily for the heart and lungs to get them functioning efficiently. Your PR readings will give you a constant check on the horse's condition.

17

COMPETING IN YOUR FIRST THREE-DAY EVENT

Preparations for a three-day event are more complicated than those required for horse trials. Be sure you meet the qualifications; three-day events require you to have completed at least four Preliminary horse trials, without cross-country penalties. It is best to have spent at least one full season at the Preliminary level before tackling the first three-day event.

There is a lot of paperwork to think about. First of all, the entry. Be sure to get it in early, as eventing is so popular now that those who put off sending in entries until the last minute find themselves on waiting lists. In the Omnibus Schedule the opening date is clearly listed. There's no point in sending an entry in any earlier because it will just be sent back or put at the bottom of the pile. So send it on the opening date. With the entry you must include a stabling form stating when you will arrive and any special needs, for example, accommodations for a stallion. You should also note if you want to be stabled next to anyone in particular. It is a good plan to get together with a couple of friends and share an extra stall as a tack room. You will be bringing a lot of equipment, and trying to work out of your trailer is difficult.

Be sure your Coggins test is up-to-date. If you are going out-of-state you should have a health certificate made out by your vet within ten days of the date you plan to leave, otherwise you might find yourself languishing on the border until the state calls a vet for you. This is time-consuming and expensive. Check with your blacksmith and have the horse shod about seven to ten days before the competition. This gives you time to make sure there are no shoeing problems.

You need somewhere to stay. If you have a camper, you can stay at the grounds; otherwise you need a motel room or a friend's house.

If the event is far away, as it might well be since there are not many Preliminary three-day events offered, you must consider going a couple of days early so that your horse has time to recover from the trip and settle in new surroundings. Travel can take a lot out of a horse. If the trip is over five hours, go at least two, preferably three, days in advance. That gives you one day in which to loaf around and two days to work before the actual competition. If you have a trip of over ten hours, plan on a halfway stop where you should get the horses out and walk them around to keep them from stiffening up too much. All these considerations can give you the edge over someone who neglects such simple precautions. If the weather has been extremely hot, it is smart to travel at night to take advantage of cooler temperatures. The horses will fare much better.

ARRIVAL

When you arrive at the show grounds, pick up your stall assignments from the stable manager and find out when the competitors' briefing will be. Get your horse settled in before you do anything else. Hang up buckets and arrange the tack room. If you are a couple of days early, you can then give the horse a drink and hack it out quietly to see the new surroundings. If you arrive the day before the competition, get your horse settled in with a haynet first, then start planning your timetable for the weekend.

FIRST VET INSPECTION

The veterinarian will examine your horse in the barn upon arrival to check for infectious diseases and general health. This is a preliminary check and not a check for soundness.

Some events hold the first veterinary check on the morning of the dressage day. Most, however, hold it the day before. Your horse should be as clean as you can get it, braided neatly and turned out in the bridle. Don't just saunter up with the horse in a halter, unbraided and dirty. Stand in front of your horse, holding a rein in each hand, while the veterinarians and ground jury inspect it at a standstill. Then trot out smartly in the designated place. Run briskly and let your horse have a fairly loose rein so the jury can see it move. When you are done, the horse goes back into its stall, the braids are taken out, and you can attend the briefing. If you have help with you, your groom can walk or lunge your horse while you attend the briefing, *but only the rider may school it once the competition has started.*

Jog for the vet inspection.

Group walking.

When walking and studying the course, too large a group can be distracting.

BRIEFING

At the competitors' briefing listen carefully and take notes. You don't want to miss anything vital. Find out where the bit and tack inspection for the dressage will be; find out where your dressage ring is; listen to any special rules pertaining to roads and tracks or cross country. Ask if you can have someone assist you after the steeplechase; ask where the vet box will be, and find out how to get there with all your equipment. Write everything down—there is really too much to remember.

COURSE INSPECTION

Organizers usually provide four-wheel-drive vehicles for the competitors for the inspection of the roads and tracks. Jump in, but be sure you have your map and pen with you. *Make a note of any mandatory flags you go through* and *number them* to be sure you don't miss any. First-time eventers often come to grief by inadvertently missing a flag. Sometimes organizers fall behind in preparations and all the markers may not be up when you do the first walk. Check *very thoroughly* to see just *how many* there will be.

The steeplechase course is usually walked on foot. Again, be sure you know just where the start is and watch the number of fences and the flags. Many mistakes are made on steeplechase at the Preliminary level. When

Julie Jones

Be sure to walk through the water to test the footing and measure the distance.

Discussing the water fence and how to tackle it.

riding this phase for the first time, it is easy to succumb to the excitement and forget what you are doing. An experienced coach would tell you the same thing.

After the steeplechase most organizers will allow grooms to wait in a designated spot, ready to throw water on the horse and check the tack and shoes in case you need help at the ten-minute break. Choose a convenient spot some distance from the finish line and make sure your groom knows where it is. Phase C, the second roads and tracks, is usually considerably longer than Phase A. Note down all the markers and make notes on your map of the actual terrain: the hills, the flat places, the rough spots. You'll be coming back again but note it down now. When you get to the end of Phase C, spend some time in the vet box. Look around for a good spot to put your equipment and ask what the procedure will be. Many vets will have you trot in on a loose rein so that they can look at your horse before you actually dismount.

CROSS COUNTRY COURSE

Walk the course with everyone else. Make a note of the direction of the course, but just use this walk as a first glance. Your actual planning will come later. Try to stay fairly near the official who is conducting the walk and

Julie Jones

Examining the bounce steps.

listen to any questions other people might ask. After your walk, return to the stable and check on your horse.

Try to keep the feeding schedule as close as possible to the one you have been using at home. At times this is difficult as everyone seems to have staggered feeding times and the horses on each side of yours may be fed at quite different hours. Try to keep a full haynet in front of the horse except on cross-country day. The water bucket must be full of clean water at all times. If it is summertime, two water buckets might be in order. Remember that you want the horse to be as relaxed and comfortable as possible.

You might want to get your horse out and do some dressage schooling after the course inspection. It will depend greatly on how the organizer has set up the timetable. If your horse is used to being turned out at home, you must allow for this and give it extra walking either by hand or riding out. If the course inspection was in the morning, you could ride soon after lunch and then do your second walking of the roads and tracks and steeplechase. *The more you walk the courses, the more certain you will be of where you are going.* I think the reason so many first-time riders go off-course is because they figure the roads and tracks are simple and don't need to be walked twice. I was guilty of that at my first three-day event. Thinking that the phases were so well marked, I never bothered to go back; went through the wrong gate, got thoroughly lost on Phase C, and, when I did find my way, had to gallop the rest of the way. I came in with 178 penalties on Phase C and my horse badly blown.

Julie Jones

Walking the course and measuring the distances. You need to know where you should be for every minute in order to make the time.

Nicely bent for a circle in the warm up.

When you walk the steeplechase for the second time, pay particular attention to the actual lay of the land—see where the hills are. Going uphill will take more out of your horse and you will want to try to ease up on the inclines. Look at the flagging and determine the shortest route. You can often save a good bit of ground by hugging the inside of the curves; the middle is not necessarily the best place to be.

Providing there is time, you should then walk the cross country again. This is the important time, as you must now decide on your plan of attack. Study each fence carefully. Plan your approaches. Think of where the sun will be when you ride and make allowances for fences that might be in shadow at that time. Try to walk with your coach or an experienced rider and listen to his or her advice. Often there are many ways of negotiating each fence. Think about your particular horse. Jot down terrain problems in your notebook. See if you can save ground anywhere. Note any muddy spots, and look carefully at the take-off sides of fences and think about what might happen if it rains before your go. Note the approximate halfway point and look for stretches where you can give your horse a breather. Study, study, study. The secret of riding successfully cross country lies in being fully prepared.

DRESSAGE DAY

Your timetable for this day will be dependent on your riding time. If you ride early, the morning will be spent grooming, braiding, lungeing and warming up. The afternoon will be devoted to more course walking. If, on the other hand, you don't ride until 1 p.m. or later, your helper can walk or lunge the horse while you go back and do a second and third walking of the cross-country course.

It is a good idea to take a measuring wheel to check the distance and to plan your course and where you will be every minute. At a speed of 520, you should note where 520 meters is on course, then 1040, then 1580, and so on so you can really be aware of how you are doing as you ride.

Walking the roads and tracks and steeplechase can be done twice. Rarely will you need to go back over these if you have made enough notations on the number of flags, etc. But the *cross country needs at least three walks and perhaps a fourth one so that you are really prepared.*

For the dressage, you want your horse looking its very best. A thorough grooming (or a bath if it is hot weather), neat braids, and spotless tack are the requirements. Allow plenty of time for your warm-up. Usually big three-day events run on time, but sometimes even the best-organized competitions get off schedule. Be sure to check with the ring stewards to see if your ring is running on time. Perform your warm-up in the designated place; there is usually a practice ring available. The custom is to warm up outside of it until there are two or three horses in front of you, then you spend the final minutes in the practice ring.

There may be more of a crowd than you are accustomed to, but don't be distracted. Your horse has done this before and your purpose is to show the horse off to all these people. Stay relaxed and don't change your routine just because this is a "big" competition. After the horse in front of you has finished and left the ring, take those few last minutes to ride around the arena. It will probably have some decorations in the way of flowers, so let your horse have a look at them. Confidence in yourself and your horse is half the battle in performing a good test. You are no longer novices and you should look relaxed and efficient. Ride the best test of your career.

When you have finished, exit the ring and take your horse back to the stables. Replace your dressage saddle with a jumping saddle, take off your coat, stock, hat and other finery, and take your horse for a final "blow out." Organizers will designate a place for galloping and you need to do a short, sharp wind sprint of about a quarter mile at steeplechase speed. This allows your horse to "blow out" its lungs, sharpening it for the next day.

The final touches—removing the bandages and checking the turn out.

Julie Jones

An ideal extended canter.

When you finish, the horse can have the rest of the day to be quiet and relax. You might want to walk it out again that evening, especially if you did ride early. Sit down with your helper and write down a "battle plan" for the next day.

PLANNING CROSS COUNTRY DAY

Your whole plan revolves around your starting time for the first roads and tracks. The horse must have its morning feed at least two hours before the start. Water should be taken out about an hour before you leave. The horse will perform better on an empty stomach than a full one, so don't feed it any hay in the morning. Allow plenty of time to tack up and to get yourself to the start of Phase A.

Your helper needs to have a list of all the equipment you will need in the vet box (see Table 5). As soon as you leave for Phase A, your things can be transported there. If you are going to have a quick break after the steeplechase, figure out exactly when you will be arriving there so your helper is ready. Your arrival back in the vet box after Phase C must also be carefully planned and your help must know when to expect you. If you have more than one helper, one can be stationed at the steeplechase course, to 1) time your go, and 2) take care of you and the horse as you come off the course. If the steeplechase course is apart from the main cross country area, it is almost imperative to have two people to help because one will have a hard time getting back and forth in time. At the end of the cross country, you will probably need about a half hour before you can start back to the stables.

CROSS COUNTRY DAY

Feed the horse according to your time schedule; groom it and take out the haynet and water bucket. Have your help take all of your vet box equipment to the vet box area. Stake out a convenient place, shady if it is hot, sheltered if it is cold. Everything should be clearly marked with colored tape in your stable colors and your initials or name. Try to be near the water supply and park uphill if it is muddy so you can get out again. If the weather is cold, fill all your buckets with water and let them stand to take the chill off. If it is very hot, you will need to fill at least two buckets with ice in the water.

If you go late in the day, you should spend the morning out on the course, watching any fence you feel particularly worried about. See how others tackle it and figure out which is the best way through any combination that puzzled you. Often a well thought-out plan has to be changed after the competition starts.

Waiting for rider and horse to come into ten minute box after Phases A, B and C.

Tack up. It is a good idea to braid the bridle into the mane. This can keep the bridle on if you should happen to come off over the horse's head. If you use an overgirth, be sure it is properly fitted and won't slip backwards. Get to the start of Phase A about five minutes before you are due to go. You don't need to take any jumps before setting out. It is good to have a piece of adhesive tape on your arm with the times of each phase written down on it. It can be quite brief:

A 3600 meters   15 min.
B 2240 meters   3 min. 30 sec.
C 5580 meters   24 min. 30 sec.
D 4330 meters   8 min. 20 sec.
(Halfway fence -13, 4 min. 10 sec.)

This will serve as a reminder and help you to keep track of your progress.
  By planning carefully, you can pick up a couple of minutes on the roads and tracks and use them as an added breather. If you can cover 1000 meters (1 km) in 4 minutes, you gain a few seconds over the required time. Most horses can cover 1 km comfortably at the trot in that amount of time. As you go along the roads and tracks, each 1000 meters will be marked: 1000 meters, 2000 meters, 3000 meters, and so on. These give you built-in check points at which you should look at your watch.

Roads and tracks—a nice trot out in the country.

When given the signal to start, punch your watch and set out at a good trot. Your horse should be feeling quite good and, if it is really pulling, try not to fight too much; rather, encourage it to relax. Singing helps pass the time.

If there is a small pile of logs along the way, you might jump them as a warm-up fence, but don't go out of your way to do so. Upon reaching the end of Phase A and the start of Phase B, pull up and check in with the starters. You should have a couple of minutes in hand. Use them to check your girths, the horse's boots, and reset your watch. Shorten your stirrups to steeplechase length and, if you feel like it, trot around a bit. If you are late coming in off A, which seldom happens, you will go directly into the starting box for steeplechase, so be prepared for this.

At the signal, set off at the gallop; *however, I would strongly caution you to take the first fence a little slower than the required speed.* Your horse isn't really ready to jump the first fence at speed. If you steady into the first one, you can increase afterwards to make up the time. Even experienced horses and riders have trouble with the first fence on steeplechase, and, for your debut, it is better to have a few time faults than to fall over the first fence. Your horse needs time to settle into a stride and it also needs to get a couple of fences under itself before catching on to the required techniques. First-time three-day riders often come to grief unnecessarily by forgetting to think.

Balanced position on course for the steeplechase

As you come off the steeplechase, let your horse slow up gradually and come down to a trot; then pull up by your prearranged check spot. Your helper can throw a bucket of water between the horse's front legs to help it cool off on Phase C, and you can have a drink or an orange to take along with you. The first part of Phase C should be devoted to letting your horse catch its breath. Allow 6 minutes for the first 1000 meters to let the horse begin recovery.

Some people get off and jog along beside the horse to help it recover, but be sure you are a good runner to do this. The practice is fraught with peril, because once you are off, it is sometimes hard to get back on again. The horses are excited and you may find that you lose a great deal more time trying to remount than you can afford. There are several cautionary tales about this. One rider got off and checked the girth, couldn't get the horse to stand still to get back on, and came in with 78 penalty points for being late. Another got off to fix a loose bandage and let go of the horse, which promptly ran off into the woods. It took five minutes to catch it again, and they got 176 penalty points. So to those who think that roads and tracks are simple: be warned to expect the unexpected!

Presuming all goes well, you should come into the vet box with a horse that is breathing easily. If you have managed to gain some time, you can

Adjusting the girth and overgirth in the ten minute box.

walk the last quarter mile or so. As you come in, the vets will want to check your horse right away. Many vets like you to trot down a specific lane so that they can see how the horse is moving. Do this, then dismount, run up your stirrups, have your help put the halter on over the bridle, loosen the noseband, undo the overgirth and loosen the girth (all this can go on while the vet is checking the temperature, pulse and respiration). Check with the starter as to exactly how much time you have. Ask the vet how your horse's PR numbers are. Then walk the horse slowly, checking the legs and shoes for anything that might need attention. Remove the boots and wash them off in the water bucket. Check the legs carefully and wash them off as well.

If the weather is hot, water—lots of it—should be used to get the horse's temperature down as much as possible. Contrary to the old fashioned belief that putting cold water on the horse's loins caused tying up, physiology studies have proved that using water all over the horse's main muscle masses does nothing but good. Sponging water is good, even better is using large towels soaked in ice water and thrown over the hindquarters and shoulders, leaving them a minute, and then removing the towels. Scraping the water off and repeating the application as many times as you can really helps to cool the horse quickly.

Do not leave the towels on for very long; you are trying to remove the built-up heat from the horse's muscles. Scrape off the warm water and apply

Julie Jones

Loosening the noseband and checking tack in the ten minute box.

more iced towels and scrape again. Leaving warm water on the horse will not cool it. Keep your horse walking as you work on it. If the weather is cold, sponge down the horse and put a cooler over it and keep it moving to avoid a chill. It is not a good idea to put a rain sheet on your horse as that would only cause it to sweat and get hotter instead of cooling off.

Meanwhile, check with other riders to see if any particular fences are causing problems. You should also ask how the ground is holding up. If it is a very wet day, and it often is, be sure to find out how the footing is and where the muddy spots are. Competitors are always helpful. That's one of the joys of eventing—everyone roots for everyone else and riders always come to each other's aid.

Keep checking the time. When you have about five minutes to go, scrape the water off, replace the boots and redo the girth and overgirth. Be sure you have your bat and gloves, remove the halter, tighten the noseband, put grease on the legs to prevent your horse from getting hung up on a fence, and check back with the vet so that he or she can give you the go-ahead. Mount up and make a last-minute check. There is quite a bit to do and not much time to do it in. This is why good help is indispensable.

Walking the horse in the ten minute box.

Check into the starting box (or just outside if you have a really excitable horse). Remember that someone can lead your horse in and stand with it until the countdown. Review the course quickly in your mind, revising any of your plans if you have heard of last minute problem obstacles. Off you go.

Your helper should then tidy up, put everything together and move over to the finish area at the end of the course.

ON COURSE

As you start, punch your watch. Ride easily to the first fence and then ride according to your plans. Above all, listen to your horse, your partner. Feel how it is holding out. Does it seem to have plenty of power left or should you throttle down? This is the true test of horsemanship; you must know your horse well enough to know just how much you can push it. If you have done your job thoroughly, a Preliminary three-day event should be no trouble at all, but if you have had troubles or setbacks in the months leading up to the event (injuries, etc.), keep that in mind and ride accordingly. This first three-day event is mileage for you and your horse. Treat it

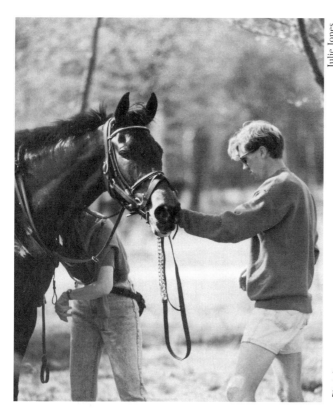

Julie Jones

The vet checking the pulse rate in ten minute box.

as such and be content to complete the competition. Don't be overly anxious to place this first time out. Save your horse for another day. Denny Emerson, a great competitive rider himself, was overheard counselling a younger rider, "Just count this one as mileage. Save him on the course. Use this as experience." This is good advice from someone who really knows eventing.

Check your watch at the halfway point. If your horse has plenty left and you are a little late, perhaps you can make up some time on the flat galloping stretches. Some courses are difficult to make the time on, some are easy. Base your strategy on how your horse feels. If you are unfortunate enough to have a fall (and everyone does at one time or another), try to hang onto the reins and get back in the saddle as quickly as possible. Jog the horse out to make sure it is sound and get back on course as fast as you can. You can't make up the lost time, but you needn't waste any more either.

At the finish, slow up gradually after passing the finish flags, first a trot, then to walk. Dismount and walk your horse back to the cooling down area.

Your horse should be cooled out carefully. The veterinarians like to recheck the horses and will have you wait at the vet area until they give permission

In the ten minute box, last minute discussion of how the course is riding

to go back to the barn. In any case, take the pulse and respiration yourself and see how quickly they come back to normal. This will tell, better than anything else, just how successful your program has been. It will also point out needed improvements for next time. Eventing at the three-day level is very different from riding in horse trials, and you must evaluate how your horse has coped with the task. The PR numbers will give you an indication of what to expect in the future.

AFTER CROSS COUNTRY

Once the horse has cooled out, it can be taken back to the barn. All of your equipment must be gathered up and brought back also. Your horse is allowed to drink as soon as it has cooled off and the haynet can be put back into the stall. The legs must be very carefully gone over for any cuts or swellings, and stable bandages put on. Many riders like to poultice after cross-country, but this depends upon the condition of the horse's legs. A good rubdown with alcohol and skillfully applied bandages serve as well as most treatments. After an hour, your horse can be offered a small feeding.

All that tack should be thoroughly cleaned and put away. The horse can be led out to graze for a while if the weather is suitable, and it should definitely be walked for 15 minutes before being trotted up in hand to check for any problems. Then it can be put away for the night. Let it relax and be quiet, but be sure to check on it at two-hour intervals.

Julie Jones

Going back to the stables after cross-country.

If there has been an injury, get the veterinarian to look at it before leaving the vet area, and have the stable vet attend to it upon return to the stable. Some horses seem prone to colic after cross country, which is why you should keep a close check on your horse's general well-being. Be sure there is plenty of fresh, clean water in the stall at all times, with electrolytes dissolved in it if the weather is hot. The exertion causes a great salt loss, which you must replace.

Provided all has gone well and the horse is resting quietly, you can go to the traditional competitors' party to celebrate. You have only one more chore. *Check your horse one final time just before you go to bed, before the stables are closed for the night.*

STADIUM DAY

Your horse should be brushed off early and walked out for at least 30 minutes before the compulsory vet check. Many horses come out a bit stiff after cross country. If this is the case with yours, you should loosen it up. If necessary, lunge it for a few minutes. The horse should then be braided again, and brought to the vet check in its bridle. The procedures are the same as

Julie Jones

The final jog.

for the first check. The veterinarians and the Ground Jury inspect each horse at a standstill, then watch it jog out for soundness.

Your horse can then go back to its stall for breakfast while you inspect the stadium course. Walk it once or twice, depending upon the length, and then get yourself ready for the final test. Usually at a three-day event there will be a parade of competitors. This may take place before the jumping or after, so be sure you know where you are supposed to be and when you are to be there—then be ready.

Take a little longer than usual to warm up. Your horse may well be feeling the effects of the day before. Be sure it is well-loosened up before you start jumping.

Find out where the presentation ceremonies will be if you have placed. At three-day events, ribbons are often presented up to ten places and sometimes all competitors who complete all three phases are called back to receive a "competition-completed" ribbon. Be sure that you know what the correct procedures are.

Your horse can then go back to the stall for a well-earned rest while you pack up your equipment for the return journey. If you live a long distance away, you should let your horse relax that night and travel the next day.

Julie Jones

Inspecting the stadium course.

Pam Olsen

The final phase.

When you get home, review the whole competition carefully. Make notes of how it went; what mistakes you made, where you could improve, and how your horse handled the entire competition. If you are lucky, things will have gone well, and you will be the proud owner of one of those rare athletes, a real three-day event horse.

TABLE 5: VET BOX EQUIPMENT LIST

3 large wash buckets (you can't have too many)
1 smaller bucket for drinking
2 large sponges
2 sweat scrapers
1 small sponge for washing out mouth
2 large towels
Sweat sheet, warm cooler (depending on weather)
Rain sheet
Extra set of shoes, with studs in. If the horse should lose one, this saves valuable time as the blacksmith can quickly tack one on without having to shape it.
Extra girth, reins, bridle, stirrup leather
Halter and lead shank
Vet emergency kit: Cotton, gauze, antiseptic, blunt scissors, adhesive tape, sponges, antibiotic dressing, bandages, 4" Elastoplast
Leather hole punch
Salt tablets and Gatorade or cold drink for rider
Extra gloves, bat, towels
Grease for legs

At end of steeplechase
Bucket of water
Sponge
Drink or fruit
Towel
Easy boot and tape, in case your horse loses a shoe